"Simple, powerful, an̲ ̲ ̲ ̲ ̲ ̲ ̲ ̲ ̲ ̲ ̲ ̲ ̲ ̲ p̲u̲r̲e̲ ̲m̲a̲g̲i̲c̲.̲ ̲I̲ ̲haven't read a book that shook me up this much since *The War of Art* by Steven Pressfield. *The Creative Wound: Heal Your Broken Art* is a must-read—and an essential tool—for creative people across the globe."
– *Lauren Sapala, author of Firefly Magic and The INFJ Writer*

"A soothing balm for your creative battle scars, this is a book for anyone who feels they have more to bring to the world but suffer doubt, feel ashamed, or wildly over-think their creativity. It gently equips you to direct your life's art with purpose and perspective, rather than allowing the pain to write for you. Happy healing!"
– *Andy Mort, musician, writer, and creator of The Gentle Rebel Podcast*

"It's real, it's relevant, it's personal, it's constructive, it's readable, and it is *not* cheesy self-help! This will be an incredibly important book to many creative people."
– *Tim Gough, award-winning leadership blogger & author*

"The Creative Wound is a book that will help you take that vital look inside, and offers great wisdom and practical tips toward rebuilding your creative foundations in a stronger, more positive way."
– *Rick Jesse, Dogtooth brand & experience design*

The Creative Wound

HEAL YOUR BROKEN ART

Mark Pierce

www.revelator.co.uk

Copyright

Contents

AUSTRALIAN MEMOIRS

ENDNOTES

Preface

I have grown through writing this book.

As I wrote about the things I've learned, I learned them more deeply.

In many ways, the pages written here are an aide memoir; things I've learned about imagination and the creative life I never want to forget; lessons I want to pass on to my daughter so she has the chance to go further, and achieve more, than I ever manage during my lifetime.

I was surprised to discover how much the journey would demand that I take big gulps of the very medicine I was busy prescribing; and as a result, I'm now a stronger and more whole man than the one who set out.

This outcome wasn't my aim, but it has served to settle my heart on the validity of sharing my thoughts and experiences here with you.

This is the best kind of journey.

My hope as you read these pages is that you, too, will emerge having been on an unanticipated adventure of the heart; one that brings you freedom, wholeness, and creative liberty in every worthy endeavour you turn your hand to.

Introduction

I ran into the garden and stood in anticipation, a plump seven-year-old yearning for a flicker of delight as I held up a drawing I'd just finished, only for my open heart to be decimated.

"Shut up, you fat bastard."

The adult whose care I was supposedly in stormed straight past without breaking stride. I ran upstairs, locked myself in the bathroom, and sobbed for an age. My artistic heart and self-worth were left gasping for air from the blow of that sentence—the inevitable right hook following years of tiresome jabs.

Those five words confirmed my suspicions: the disinterest and disdain toward me and my creativity were real, and the wraps were now completely off so I no longer needed to wonder.

This was the moment my relationship with creativity changed, the point it finally tipped.

I had no name for it back then, but this is my clearest early memory of what I now refer to as a Creative Wound. This is the infliction of damage to the core of who we are as creators. It is an attack on our artistic identity, resulting in us believing that whatever we make is somehow tainted or invalid, because shame has convinced us there is something intrinsically tainted or invalid about ourselves. This is the older brother of the imposter syndrome. Self-doubt on steroids. It is rooted deeper, and seems more true, than plain uncertainty.

Rather than permitting us the joy of plunging into the ocean of our untapped potential, a Creative Wound restricts us to a life splashing around in the shallows. Yes, it is safer, but it lacks any of the exhilaration we truly long for in our art.

A Creative Wound has the power to delay our pursuits— sometimes for years—and it can even derail our lives completely. This may sound melodramatic, but really it's not. Anything that makes us feel ashamed of ourselves or our work can render us incapable of the self-expression we yearn for.

On that afternoon in March 1980, I had no idea a long career as a creative professional hung precariously in the balance, but, aged seven, I was already punch-drunk, emotionally spent, and felt as if giving up might be my best option. However, in that moment, my young self knew I had to push against the crushing; and so, as more assaults came, the more I pushed.

I pushed *hard.*

Today, I get to play, record and produce music; I shoot photos for album covers, magazine editorial features, and stylised imagery for interesting people and brands; I design album artwork and book covers; I consult on marketing and brand direction for small businesses, and I coach fellow creatives. Oh, and I write.

Had resignation got the better of me that day in 1980, and I'd failed to approach my life and work with gritty imagination, I'd never be doing all that I enjoy today. Some of it, maybe. But certainly not all of it.

Every day I meet gifted people who are unable to share the brilliance that lives inside them because they are frightened or in too much pain. I'm thankful I've avoided joining the many who've abandoned their art in exchange for apparent safety. I'm not famous, nor do I aspire to be, but I do get to make things that make a difference. I'm living the life of my own design, and so can you.

Whether success for you means forging a full-time career in the arts, or simply being able to enjoy exploring your imagination without the companionship of debilitating emotions, this book will instil creative courage in you. Through it, you will recover your creative confidence if you've lost it, or finally discover your creative heart if you're yet to determine where it lies.

CREATIVE DERAILMENT & RESTORATION

In what follows, I will define what Creative Wounds are, how they happen, and discover ways they have been derailing your artistic life. Then together we will investigate methods of solving the persistent problems they create and learn how to get free of their hindrance so you can spend your time making art instead of drifting along in frustration.

Some books promise a step-by-step formula to the secret of creative bliss. This isn't one of those. That whole 'painting-by-numbers' approach to art has never resonated with me. Consequently, I don't have prescriptive methods to my work, and I refuse to cheat you by fabricating any here. Instead, I am offering you insight into *a way*—a pointing of the compass and an exposition of the terrain. This will help you establish a posture of heart and clarity of mind with which to guide your creative life.

My aim is to put tools into your hands and ideas into your head so you can experience restored wholeness and confidence in relation to your creative world.

I write from first-hand experience gained from a long career as a professional multi-disciplined creative. During my time with a series of UK design and branding agencies, I would repeatedly find myself being the unofficial studio counsellor/coach. This was when I discovered I had a knack for pinpointing how an individual had become creatively stuck. I would then help them work through the necessary process so they could return to an enjoyable and productive creative flow.

There was no on-the-job guidance for doing this, so in my own time I devoured scores of books and courses, and trained myself so that I could help my friends and colleagues more effectively.

The same pattern continues to this day within my own business, which I started in 2005. Scores of my creative clients have first needed restoration and renewed courage before we could effectively work on their project with any real freedom. And helping people with this internal work is far more important to me than simply turning a quick profit. Plus, I've discovered this approach is more profitable in the long-term anyway, as I've suffered far fewer abandoned projects as a result. Artists who pursue wholeness tend to grow in confidence rather than quitting in a panic part way through.

Because I understand the crippling nature of Creative Wounds, and have healed from them many times over the years, I am able, with heartfelt empathy, to take stuck people by the hand and walk them through a journey of reclaiming their creativity. This is where the idea for this book came from and what forms its basis.

For over two decades, I have drawn from the streams of psychology and spirituality and stood alongside fellow creatives in the trenches of their personal and professional battles until they secured their individual victories. Beyond artmaking, much of my creative life and work has involved diving into the mud and blood of this invisible war zone to pull people out. Survival and restoration from the brutality of a Creative Wound is a real thing, and I want you to stay creatively alive. So I offer you my perspective and the best lessons I've learned so far, along with suggested approaches I've seen bring undeniable transformation.

THE AIMS OF THIS BOOK

This book is a manifesto for helping you reclaim your deepest expressive longings. It's a rallying cry to those who have suppressed, ignored, or covered-over their dream of being creatively fruitful, to not let that dream die on the vine—as what a travesty *that* would be.

If creativity and pain are synonymous to you, be assured you are not alone. Using the guidance in these pages you will be able to locate the specific moments in which you were wounded and knocked off course. You'll also gain valuable new insight into what your *real* beliefs are, and how to cultivate more of the good and eliminate the toxic ones that serve only to poison your creative life.

This book is divided into three parts. The first focuses on the importance and impact of your contribution and why your creative life matters.

The second part defines what a Creative Wound is and explains how to locate the roots of your Creative Wounds.

The third part teaches you my most effective methods for changing course back onto your true creative path, bringing with it a dramatic transformation of your entire experience.

Each chapter revolves around a single resounding theme: it is entirely possible to overcome whatever is currently holding you back from doing your best creative work.

So if you'll dare to open the door a crack, and peep out from within the safe haven you and your creativity are hiding, I've got some good things to share with you.

It's time to heal your broken art.

[PART 1]

WHY YOUR CREATIVE LIFE MATTERS

There are people who need the very thing you've been holding back.

Why Make Art?

Art exists to remind us that we are alive. It reminds us that we are human, that we each have a soul. An artist creates magic from the mundane and leads us by the hand into another world, or more deeply into the one we're in.

To make art is to make something from the truth as you see it. Real art is a gift that establishes a connection or inspires transformation, first to you as the maker and then to anybody else you invite to share in it.

Art is made by ordinary people. Brilliant, weird, imperfect, reasoning, feeling, thinking, normal, everyday people. These are people who choose to live deeply and have grown tired of a life doing things that mean nothing.

Art isn't about following instructions and making what you're told to make. Neither is it about being able to copy, even if you copy well.

The medium you choose doesn't make your work a work of art, and demonstrating a high skill level doesn't automatically make you an artist.

But if you've stirred a heart, changed a mind, or uncloaked a mystery, *then* you've made something worthy of the name.

ART IS ABOUT LIFE

There's a bigger concept to grasp here than just wanting to master a particular technique, and a more pertinent question to be answered than "will anyone like this?" Our creative work is more significant than we think, because it rarely takes place in a vacuum and is part of a much larger story than we realise is unfolding at the time.

Art—real art—isn't actually *about* art. It's about life.

Let me explain.

In the hallway of my mum's home there hangs a framed landscape, painted by my grandma back in 1979. She has long since passed, but every time I visit home I get to re-experience a moment, a snapshot in time Grandma saw. It captures a dramatic scene in the Scottish Highlands: the fire of the sun ignites the thick, brooding clouds with its rich, red flame, which in turn blanket the peaks of the imposing mountains, as another day concludes in spectacular fashion.

Curiously, it seems almost an extravagant waste of beauty as the only audience present to admire its glory that day was this one solitary artist. But in reality, it was far from a squandering, as this painting is inseparable from what Grandma's eyes saw, what her soul experienced, and what her hands created. And because of this, something of her personhood lives on.

You see, that's not just a painting hanging in Mum's hallway. It's the very life essence of an artist, a mother, a wife, a grandmother—now permanently encapsulated in oil on a small, canvas board.

In the years to come, I'm looking forward to telling my daughter all about this painting and of her great grandma, as the two are intrinsically linked. This landscape is now a bridge across time that spans four generations and is far more than just a nice rendition of a piece of Scottish scenery; it's evidence of a creative soul in particular who once spent time on planet earth. It is evidence of someone who mattered, and, indeed, still does.

For ourselves and future generations to flourish we must take our creativity back, because to crush original thought and personal expression is to crush an individual's spirit. You are almost certainly reading this book because you know artistry matters beyond surface aesthetics, and you're aware there is a contending over yours. So, let us choose to fight fiercely for our creative hearts, not for the love of war, but for the love of what we'd lose if we surrender.

Art—real art—isn't actually *about* art.

It's about life.

WHY EVEN BOTHER?

I find the reasons people create art fascinating, especially given the large investment of time and commitment it can demand. Developing proficient skills and learning the nuances of your chosen field is usually a lifetime labour of love. Plus, as so much wonderful art has already been created by insanely gifted people, it begs the question— why even bother?

Let me tell you a few stories that might help you answer the question for yourself.

I have friends in Finland who spent two years living in the UK. One morning, they emailed me to share how their eight-year-old son refuses to sleep unless my album *Catapult* is playing. At first I thought I might have stumbled across a musical cure for insomnia, but instead I learned that my songs, and one in particular, called *Sing*, would bring him to tears as he recalled happy memories that reawakened his longing for England.

There is a Welsh word that encompasses this feeling better than any English ones I know: *hiraeth*. This is a feeling of homesickness tinged with sadness over the lost or departed—a mix of longing, yearning, nostalgia, and wistfulness.

This seemed to be what my friends' little boy was experiencing.

I wrote *Sing* years before I moved to North Wales or had ever heard of *hiraeth*, and long before Finland had any part in my life. Plus, I had no idea that writing it would help a Finnish boy process the events and feelings of his young life. But I'm glad I did, and I'm glad it helped.

That's why I make art.

A few days before getting my Finnish friends' email, I visited a local hospice in relation to a project I was working on. Here, I met a lady who also owned a copy of my album. Actually, I discovered she'd bought multiple copies, and had distributed them widely to friends and family. As we chatted, she relayed anecdote after anecdote about her relationship with my music, climaxing with the one where a song of mine had helped her son process the story of his life, and in which he'd ended up marrying the woman of his dreams! I've no idea quite how I managed to help with that, but a few simple chords and words I'd written and recorded had again made a positive difference to somebody somewhere.

That's why I make art.

The hospice project I mentioned was to arrange and record a memorial song, co-written by a group who had all recently lost someone close to them. It was humbling to help these precious, grieving people record their voices, as in turn each sung their tribute to a loved one who would never get to hear it. I'm glad they couldn't see me fighting back tears.

I think I was the only one crying, though, because what could have been a sombre or overwhelming experience erupted into nothing short of joy as riotous laughter became the theme of our studio sessions.

Writing and recording this song helped these wonderful people process a devastating chapter in the story of their lives.

That's why I make art.

My little girl is just over two years old at the time of writing. She has a fast-developing vocabulary, including a few fun words she's made up herself. My wife, Sarah, and I regularly make up silly songs, and a particular favourite is made entirely from a word our daughter invented. Sometimes we spontaneously break out into that song while sitting round the table together. The era of this song may soon be gone as our daughter grows, so missing this moment isn't an option. It's her song. Her words. And we copy her dance moves. All three of us sing and wave our arms as exuberantly as we can, and our little girl bounces in her chair, laughing and singing—even after Sarah and I have stopped.

That's why I make art.

Art. Music. Words. They have a timeless, almost holy, power to carry the essence of our stories. They connect lonely hearts together within a community of understanding, and let others on the journey know, "You are not alone."

Yes, every chord has been played before and every story theme explored, but not by you. That's what makes it interesting. Your perspective is unique. Your touch and imprint will never be repeated. Your art can quench a thirst or nourish a soul in ways nobody else's can. But it can only do so if you let it live.

Admittedly, in creating anything you inevitably risk open criticism, and it does take hours of hard, focused, determined work to become proficient.

It is all risk. Undoubtedly.

But if we choose to risk nothing, we actually risk everything. We risk never knowing what we were capable of. We risk our innate genius dying before it ever had the chance to live. We risk being left behind.

What would your life be like if all the risks you're avoiding actually paid off? Can you recall times when art, whether your own or another artist's, swept you up into feeling part of something bigger? Wouldn't you like to have more similarly transcendent, connected moments, more frequently, and maybe even create some for others?

That's why I make art.

Where Does The Art Go?

Celebrated Spanish artist Picasso is quoted as saying "Every child is an artist. The problem is how to remain an artist once we grow up."[1]

What happens to us as we reach adulthood? Why does the art stop? Is it a natural result of human maturity or the influence of something more insidious?

There are hundreds, thousands, millions of us dormant. Musicians, poets, writers, and dancers. Filmmakers, painters, photographers, and designers. Crafters, sculptors, potters, jewellers, and orators. All gone into hiding. Diminished. Scared.

Why is that?

The answer for many of us is that we've been wounded. Wounded by friends and wounded by enemies. Our work has been rejected by authorities and disdained by the system we find our lives caught up in, a culture in which creativity is tolerated not celebrated.

Standardised education continues to churn out worker bees, prefabricated for conformity not curiosity. We are schooled to believe our tutors know all the answers, and our place is simply to memorise all we're being spoon-fed. Then we can tick all the right boxes, to pass all the right exams, so we can be deemed fit enough to be harnessed to the plough by people who have already done the thinking on our behalf—people who will readily dictate to us the path they think our lives should take, and feed us into whichever system has deemed us the most useful.

When your creativity is shut down, so is your freedom to think clearly, to reason freely, and to offer imagination and innovation to our world. And don't be fooled, you are easier to control if you stop believing that you are creative. It's no wonder imagination is beaten down in some circles.

What if you having a different idea or new expression risks unleashing a fracas? It might, because for some this is fighting talk. If you're a replaceable cog in someone else's machine, and the machine owner insists on being the one who always knows the most, it's unlikely they will entertain your ideas with much receptivity or enthusiasm. When your creative freedom threatens the status quo of the group, causes a disruption by showing a better way, or highlights the mundanity of someone else's own existence, then resistance toward your imagination and art can result, along with almost inevitable wounding.

This brings to mind the common behaviour of crabs collected in a bucket. If one crab makes a break for freedom the others often grab it and pull it back down into the group. Whether this is to thwart the escape, or an attempt to climb out on the back of the potential escapee, is open to debate. But the result is the same. Nobody escapes, because rather than lifting each other up, the group actively opposes every break-out attempt.

Take note of how many people in your life exhibit similar behaviour toward you—dragging you down rather than lifting you up. Well-meaning voices will tell you to stop complaining, be thankful, and comply with the status quo.

But are they right?

IS IT RIGHT TO BE A LUDDITE?

The Luddites were a group of textile workers from 19th century England. They violently opposed the mechanisation of the mills in which they worked because these technological advancements threatened their jobs. It was an aggressive uprising in which they destroyed machinery and burned mills.

Such was the impact of their revolt, the term Luddite has survived for over 200 years and is now commonly used to describe a technophobe—someone who struggles to operate, or ethically agree with the impact of, advancing technology.

However, it's not so much technology that's the problem,

but rather our belief that we are inherently uncreative and must resign ourselves to serving a pre-ordained system we had no part in choosing. That is the issue. And it becomes more pointed as the unrelenting development in technology continues to threaten livelihoods, shape our way of being, and dictate how we relate to the world.

Adapting to constant change demands more from us every day. And as this revolution gathers pace, we must cultivate an unprecedented agility of mind and heart—the precise traits a Creative Wound hampers.

The ability to bend with the pressure of ceaseless developments is vital because, unlike in previous generations where a job for life was commonplace, many of us will have multiple careers during our lives, some even at the same time.

Andy Mort is a great example of this. He is a respected blogger, podcaster, and speaker in the area of introversion and highly sensitive creatives. He is also an acclaimed songwriter and live performer. Plus, he is an undertaker. *An undertaker?* Which school teaches you *that* combination?

It makes perfect sense, though, when you consider the subtext of Andy's life. He is a deeply empathetic man who has a desire to connect with, and help, others. So if we consider his work supporting an online community for introverts and highly sensitive creatives, and then listen carefully to his song lyrics, and finally note how he offers strength and care to grieving families, everything becomes clear—empathy is the thread woven throughout all that Andy invests himself into.

Being creatively engaged with labour that has significant meaning to the individual is a huge factor to living a successful and fulfilling life.

COMPUTERS AND CREATIVITY

We live in an era where computerisation is an unavoidable part of modern, western culture, and because of this the role of the artist is becoming ever more vital. The ability to think creatively is a large part of what distinguishes us as being human. But the opportunity for personal creative expression is diminishing for many of us in our daily work, as much of what we produce is now template-driven homogeneity, run by computers and assembled by robots.

Of course, businesses reap the financial reward of being able to create products ever faster and cheaper, but at what cost?

For many individuals, the self-esteem that used to come from contributing to society by crafting something by hand, and in person, has all but gone from their lives.

Back in the 1960s, the mechanised vision of the future sounded blissful and exciting—promising a time when practical, manual work would become a thing of the past as machines made it unnecessary. But, as this increasingly becomes our present-day reality, we have to admit this advancement has stripped us of our souls. We are passive. And bored.

Because of this assault on our unique, individual contributions to the world, art is fast becoming one of the last bastions of human creative expression. It is vital for connecting us back to our own personal humanity and keeping alive our alliance with one another.

Vision, artistry, and individual expression are intrinsically human traits, and it is imperative that we don't concede ours. We desperately need it.

In many ways I fully support the use of technology as an aid to creativity because it allows whole new genres and careers to emerge. Without it, we'd not have such iconic movies as *Toy Story, The Matrix* or *Lord Of The Rings,* and we'd never get to hear music unless it was being performed live. All our passport pictures would be hand-drawn in pencil, and you wouldn't be reading this book, because printing wouldn't exist. Or eBooks.

Technology has given us much to be thankful for. But what would happen if we handed over our artistry entirely to machines?

We've had the benefit of spell checkers in word processing software for decades. This technology has advanced further into analysing and correcting grammar. (I used grammar and spell checkers while writing this book and am thankful for the help). But what would the future be like if the words we read were all written by computers?

It sounds far-fetched and more like sci-fi than real life, but it is already happening. In Japan, a novel written using artificial intelligence was short-listed for the Nikkei Hoshi Shinichi Literary Award prize. And since 2014, artificial intelligence has been allowed to enter the competition alongside human authors.[2]

Computers are competing against humans and being awarded prizes for creativity. Artificial intelligence is writing words for humans to read. How does that make you feel? Ought there be a cut-off point?

Granted, it is an impressive advancement to be able to share grammar rules and the rudiments of storytelling with a computer, and a coherent tale be created. Although, having read some examples of computer generated stories, I did find them a little soulless. The vital ingredient of spirit was noticeably absent—that complex, human-infused essence we get from marinading thoughts and experiences within the deep dish of our organic subconscious.

But where computerisation has succeeded—reducing the manual and mundane—it affords us space for the innovative, imaginative, and relational. I'm not saying everyone ought to be great with a brush and canvas but rather that creativity and artistry is a state of mind we're all at liberty to embrace. The years ahead will be very different to what has gone before, and intuitive, ingenious, human thinking will be crucial in how it plays out.

Best-selling author Daniel Pink has clear thoughts on this

subject: "The future belongs to a very different kind of person with a very different kind of mind—creators and empathizers, pattern recognizers, and meaning makers."[3]

The mind is a gift we dare not concede to the seemingly omniscient, omnipresent behemoth of artificial intelligence, which, while offering undeniable advantages in terms of accuracy and speed, offers us nothing of shared meaning to nourish the soul.

A TRUER MIRROR

Of the guitars I own, my favourite is a Fender Road Worn '60s Stratocaster in Olympic White. This characterful instrument bears numerous scuffs and dents, which often cue conversation with studio visitors. Aggressive dings and scrapes cut through the yellowing paint, revealing flashes of the alder body beneath. Its marred appearance alludes to decades of workmanlike service out on the road, possibly on tour with a bluesman troubadour as he bounced between honkey-tonks strewn along the route from Memphis to Chicago.

However, in reality, my Strat is only a few years old and was artificially aged before it left the factory in Mexico. I know—it's a bit of a letdown, isn't it? It hasn't actually lived the life its guise would have you believe, despite the convincing look, and there are no interesting stories behind the scars.

But even so, I still love it because it succeeds in being evocative, and it bolsters my fascination with anything that implies an unapologetic life. This guitar inspires songs, and its appearance provokes a pointed question: "How did you come to look like you do?"

Despite its sweet sound, this beautifully playable instrument is irrevocably flawed. And yet, despite the battering it has endured, it refuses to give up, insisting instead on making yet more music.

Truthfully, this guitar is a more effective mirror to me than the one in the bathroom. It offers the kind of reflection we artists need—casting back to us reminders of our resilient non-surrender in the face of terrible resistance, and of love and acceptance toward our most unsightly cracks and painful collapses.

So, perhaps a polished surface shouldn't be the goal after all. Despite us wishing it weren't the case, hardship can work in us to reveal a deeper hidden beauty: namely the marks, bruises, and signs of wear that make us—and our creativity—undeniably, exquisitely, human.

This idea is clearly demonstrated in the recording studio. When mixing music, I often reach for software plug-ins that emulate the imperfect sound of decades-old analogue equipment. Magnetic tape, transistors, and tubes—used to capture and process sound before the advent of computer recording—frequently introduced subjectively pleasing limitations and irregularities to the music.

During the era in which this hardware was cutting edge, engineers fought to maintain the cleanest signals possible.

But, as we look back, it was the unavoidable colourisation of the sound from these elements that helped give the era its sublime, irresistible and nostalgia-inducing magic. I am one of many who revere '70s music due, in part, to the tonality imparted by the equipment.

So, even though we strive to improve our skill, and edge ever closer to perfect execution, we daren't ignore the biggest trend in creative software across all disciplines, which is to purposefully add distortion and noise to technically perfect source material. Adding such irregularities creates a more organic, human feel that we seem to find more relatable and easier to love.

So, as we learn to lose the fear of offering imperfect work, our art will demonstrate its innate power to infuse meaning, inspiration, and consolation into thirsting human hearts who are in need of the very thing we've been holding back.

[PART 2]

DEFINE & LOCATE YOUR CREATIVE WOUNDS

Become a student of your own story to discover why your art is broken.

When Creativity Freezes

It's something you've known all your life: you were born to make art. For the longest time, your deep desire has been to paint, or sing, or dance, or write. You don't need me to tell you where your great passion lies. But, like the proverbial deer caught in the headlights, you have frozen—stranded within a nightmare. It's as if the sleep terrors of childhood have breached the boundaries of time and consciousness, bursting, without invitation or warning, into the living now. The perpetual winter of Lewis's Narnia has entrenched itself deep within the foundations of your artistic spirit and…

You. Just. Can't. Move.

You can't even start. Whether that means showing up at the easel, or the piano, picking up your pencil, or lifting a camera up to your eye, you're petrified by the fear of an unwelcome reacquaintance with gut-wrenching dread.

Making a fool of yourself seems inevitable. What if you do try, who knows just how bad it could go?

Fear stops the trying and leaves you with nothing but the longing.

You're aware this is some kind of self-expression paralysis, and you may even find it difficult to describe the experience. Consequently, you've suffered in silence, perhaps for a long time. Yet deep down, you know if this damage would only heal then freedom of movement would return and you'd discover all you were truly capable of.

As artists, we put our heart and soul into what we do. It's the seat of all our work. But if our heart freezes, we lose all creative power. In these moments we must abandon technique, and work directly on the essence of who we are. So, rather than discussing particular creative disciplines or the latest tips and trends, we must focus on getting unstuck on the inside; because tools and techniques are never the most important thing, but rather the creative strength and agility of the soul that wields them.

CREATIVE WOUNDS DEFINED

Life ought to come with a disclaimer: "Warning! Pain is inevitable."

I've met a lot of damaged souls. We all have. Wounds can happen in any area we make contact with the world or people; physical, emotional, spiritual, sexual, psychological. A Creative Wound occurs when an event, or someone's actions or words, pierce you, causing a kind of rift in your soul. A comment—even offhand and unintentional—is enough to cause one. Someone's indifference toward your artistic offering, which may seem innocuous, can cause the searing of your artistic heart. This kind of encounter profoundly affects how we perceive and relate to our creativity.

Consider your relationship style toward your art for a moment. Is it one of continuing celebration and honour? Or, if you're honest, do you lean more toward an attitude of contempt, derision, and cynicism?

As we look more closely at our relationship with creativity, we see not only something of our desires and personality but also the invisible wounds we carry. The source of these wounds are often found in ill-disposed opposition toward us expressing something of beauty and worth:

Nobody shows up to see your first stage appearance.

Someone sniggers and points while you are singing.

A sibling scrawls all over your best painting.

These are Creative Wounds.

My friend Rob is a fine violinist who plays in his local Philharmonic Orchestra, but for decades he's battled to silence the mocking ghost of a bandleader from his childhood, who repeatedly called his violin a "vile din".

Just a bit of fun? Not really. These were violent words against the sensitive, creative heart of a child.

PLAYING THE PART, LACKING THE HEART

The yearning to produce something of worth is a legitimate human desire, and yet it puts significant demands on us. We agitate our innermost self then synthesise it with memories, experiences, and longings. Finally, these delicate and disparate aspects of our soul are fused together so that complete strangers can critique and dissect them at will. Even for the most self-confident individual, this is a tender act. And, when we dare to expose the contents of our soul in such an unguarded manner, we invariably leave ourselves wide open to the possibility of harm.

So we hide.

And we act.

In ancient Greece, theatrical stage performances were given from behind masks—each a representation of the character they were playing. Every role was portrayed by an actor holding a disguise in front of their real face.

If we've received a significant wounding, we can often resort to this same type of role play, hiding our true selves while performing from the other side of a mask. Taking our behavioural cues from achievers we admire we're able to fool a lot of people for a long time, especially if we craft our mask with care, and hone our acting skills. We play out a version of the role we know we should be living, and try to appease our conscience by getting a taste of it without having to become the real thing.

The work we produce while living this double life is also chronically unsatisfying, due to our offerings being filtered through the persona we've adopted instead of our truest selves. It is much easier to create work that is nothing more than a rehash of what is currently popular, socially acceptable, or commercially viable, than aiming for what is an honest representation of who we actually are. This can be a safe approach for earning a living but is usually ineffective when charged with building a satisfyingly creative life. Even though the "actor's mask" can provide a buffer from the pain of aggressive critique, it also insulates us from being able to receive genuine praise—stealing away any chance of connecting with those who would love our authentic work. It is entirely possible to play the part but lack the heart.

THE BATTLE SCARS ON TIM'S GUITAR

Tim is an award-winning leadership blogger and published author. He received a significant Creative Wound as a teenager, which led to him adopting an "actor's mask" in certain situations. Here is his story:

For me, music has been a continual source of rage and disappointment. There is deep-set enmity between music and me; we have become bittersweet lovers.

When I was about fourteen, my oldest brother, tired of my incessant attempts to sound like Noel Gallagher, took my guitar from me and slid it onto the shed roof. I remember in the rawest parts of my core exactly what red acrylic polymer coating sounds like as it is dragged over galvanised zinc shingles. I remember exactly how many battle scars were on that guitar's back when it was returned to me by my parents. Most specifically, I remember the hate.

I am that guitar. I have nearly two decades of trying and trying and trying to make music work, with very little encouragement and even less success. The only people who have shown me any positive reinforcement are my wife and one or two close friends. This is largely because they are now the only people who I will let onto the field. Most people I keep outside in the Green Zone, showing them only the silly songs or purposely bad impersonations.

During the process of this kind of emotional shattering, it is common to make inner vows simply to survive the moment. These promises we make to ourselves are an attempt to take back control and provide some form of security against further damage. But all too often they limit and inhibit all future attempts at creativity. Quite appropriately, during an assault, our self-protection mode is turned on, but problems occur when the switch gets jammed.

The effects of indifference and contempt toward Tim's early musical forays have continued to shape his relationship with music, even twenty years on. He made a vow that only trusted individuals could hear his real music. Everyone else gets *the mask*. They don't hear the real music from Tim's heart, they're only allowed to hear the comedy. The evidence of a Creative Wound is easy to spot once you know his story, but without that insight you could wrongly presume Tim's main thing is silly songs.

The wound. The mask. The limitation. The frustration.

SMALL WOUNDS MATTER IN A BIG WAY

Media companies today are masters at broadcasting the world's most traumatic events direct to our homes, offices, and now even our pockets. It's almost impossible to avoid hearing of the most heinous crimes, tragic accidents, and deplorable acts of cruelty our world has to offer. It would help us to remember that media companies are just that—companies. They need to make money to survive, and bad news is often the easiest to sell. Sensationalism brings attention and customers.

It's no wonder we are becoming desensitised—which is a natural coping mechanism after all—to the end we now think nothing of being entertained by tragedy, war and gore as the content of our Friday night movie, supposedly to help us unwind after a busy week.

Tragically, because of this overexposure, we can consider our personal wounds unworthy of serious attention. By comparison, they don't seem of headline-level severity, so we suppress and ignore the pain.

Meanwhile, with every undermining comment or difficult event we endure, our identity and confidence are eroded;

and we daren't speak up because our story seems so petty compared to the extremity of the news.

Furthermore, a sense of shame often accompanies the fact a wound even happened in the first place—an awful awareness that something wrong happened, something that violated honour and mocked goodness. It is the agony of innocence being taken away by force.

And this is all compounded years later when you admit to yourself the gnawing in your soul is still present.

For a while, you consider sharing your story with others, but you don't; because doing that might verify the fear that you really *are* oversensitive, too intense, and don't have what it takes to create meaningful work that matters.

And so it builds. Layer upon layer upon layer.

Finally, you surmise that the only reasonable course of action is to rationalise, and ultimately trivialise, the damage done to you.

"I'll get over it. It doesn't matter."

But it does matter. It's serious. And it is insidious in its silence.

JUST BE MORE

I remember being in an appraisal meeting at a particular design agency I worked for, and my boss encouraging me with the four immortal words, "Just be more confident!"

I pictured him managing a football club, "Just score more goals!", or coaching a team in a dance competition, "Just dance better!"

Incredibly unhelpful.

A similar thing happened to my artist friend Julia; a quiet, sensitive soul, with a rich internal world that few recognise. She shared with me a story of her college days when her tutor's attempt at encouragement set her back significantly.

At first, it seemed innocuous.

In fact, she even agreed with the assessment.

Her tutor told Julia that the paintings she did were "exciting" but lacked refinement. At the time, she felt pretty good because he had noticed her potential, but the second part of the equation has stayed with her for years. She says, "I think at the time I agreed with it. But years later, those words remained stuck in my mind, and I guess they made me feel a little hopeless because I didn't know how to get 'more refined.'"

Criticism or critique without guidance or mentorship can easily lead to a Creative Wound so subtle that it's hard to even notice. Without a guide, the wounds of critique compound. And without grace, the truth just cuts and leaves you to bleed.

What would you think of a sports coach who berated a top athlete for being too slow when the athlete was suffering a broken leg? Not much, I'd bet. Yet we are often guilty of coaching ourselves as harshly as this.

Believing that you're lazy simply because you've not produced as much as you're capable of is rarely helpful and usually not even true. The problem is most likely not laziness but brokenness. The blows of the past have left you with a limp, and it's not more effort or discipline you need, but restoration.

Creative Wound Stories

Our lives are governed by the implicit memories of our most formative events. They act as guiding stars for our more fleeting, conscious thoughts; this is our mind's continuous sub-conscious foundation, and the basis on which we frame conscious thoughts. I liken this to the operating system of a computer, which is the framework within which every other program is used. Without an operating system, nothing else can work. So what happens if the operating system has hidden programming errors or contracts a malicious virus?

On our computers, anti-virus software serves as a guardian against malicious attacks. However, anti-virus applications are still fallible, especially if we are duped into accepting a virus in the first place. If a virus known as a *rootkit* gets past our protection and into the operating system, an anti-virus program can't help; it might even report that nothing is wrong despite our computer's obviously weird behaviour.

At this point we need something more fundamental than anti-virus software offers. We need something that penetrates deep within the core infrastructure in order to find the source of the malaise: we need a *rootkit remover*.

When healing the operating system of our creative lives, stories serve as our rootkit remover.

As we open ourselves up to interact with the stories of our lives, we unearth and give language to matters of great depth and importance. If we aspire to take our creativity back, our hidden places must be seen and heard. Engaging our stories helps us become consciously aware of what we sub-consciously accept to be true. These may be beliefs we have never been able to put words around before, and brain science explains why we find this so difficult.

Neural specialists confirm that trauma—because that's what a Creative Wound is—shuts down the left frontal lobe within the brain, which is the area that controls our language capabilities. Psychologist Dan Allender describes this in *Healing The Wounded Heart* "Literally, during trauma, language goes offline. The loss of functionality in this area is similar to the way stroke patients lose their ability to form recognizable words and speak."[1]

Consequently, in the aftermath of a traumatic event we can find it hard to accurately describe what happened to us. So, while being overwhelmed by intense feelings, it is common to have few immediate words with which to articulate the events that lie at the source of our pain.

Perspective and meaning prove elusive and we are left feeling lost and powerless.

This is when the use of story becomes a potent tool for helping us regain our lost power. Here we can make use of a familiar framework to rediscover buried memories and important forgotten details, and find suitable words to express the damaging events that have hindered our capacity to create.

As renowned trauma specialist Bessel Van Der Kolk says, "As long as you keep secrets and suppress information, you are fundamentally at war with yourself…The critical issue is allowing yourself to know what you know. That takes an enormous amount of courage."[2]

LIGHT IN THE SHADOWS

Whenever we meet with friends or family, it's never long before we start swapping stories. And when honoured with appropriate receptivity, hearing the stories of others awakens the stories of our own—trading tales of what we've done, where we've been, how it felt, and what it meant. This brings us together and unites us as people. It's a big part of being human.

Stories also help to illuminate dark places. What we choose to share when we tell our stories reveals a great deal to us about our own heart. So here, I am retelling some of my own stories to help you rediscover yours, and to demonstrate how we might engage effectively with the narrative of our creative lives.

I've withheld more damning incidents than the ones I write here, because my aim is not to condemn particular individuals or to exact any form of revenge; nor is it an exercise in self-pity. But I want to show you that I, too, have suffered the indignity of more than one Creative Wound, and hope that, in my sharing, it brings you a degree of comfort and hope. Truly you are not alone.

THE FALLIBILITY OF MEMOIR

Memoirs are never complete and seldom expose the entire truth. My stories here are as accurate as I remember them, but as many happened as a child, I'm sure I didn't fully understand everything going on around me. So, even though I'm writing with as much honesty and integrity as I know how, my words come from memory and are primarily emotional recollections of incidents that marked my soul. Ultimately, whether the facts are faultlessly recalled is immaterial. We all live from the truth of how we've interpreted our experiences, not necessarily from the accuracy of the facts.

So, with that said, onto my stories:

THE BROKEN FRAME

In many ways, the movie *Billy Elliott* reminds me of my upbringing. The year is 1984, and the synopsis is of a boy growing up in a tough working-class town in County Durham, northern England. Billy defies the prevalent macho bias to pursue his dream of being a ballet dancer.

Although I'm anything but a dancer, *Billy Elliott* provides a reference I can point to and say, *like that*, rather than trying to describe my boyhood in abstract terms. This is especially true regarding the misunderstandings Billy suffered living in a culture that offered no place for the kind of artistry he loved. Melvin Burgess's tale offers me language to better understand and express my own struggle.

The town I grew up in had little culture and finesse, and the schools I attended were not the most celebrated. In fact, my particular year was often berated for being the most unruly in living memory. So, you can imagine how I fared—a sensitive, creative, emotionally aware and gentle-spirited individual surrounded by the questionable virtues of drink, drugs, illicit sex, profanity, and the infliction of damage (on objects or people) with as much frequency as possible. I wasn't exactly at home there.

This is the broken frame within which my creative life developed.

ART ATTACK

Art and music have always been my thing; and even though I was competent at most academic subjects, I really came alive in the arts. I could even convert my talent into money—drawing the cool American cars from *Starsky & Hutch* or *The Dukes Of Hazard* for the boys, or cute puppies and kittens for the girls, which I would sell for pennies during the breaks between lessons. I was never going to retire on the proceeds but it helped with my snack funds, nonetheless.

Despite being a quiet student, my work caught the attention of the music and art departments, and they regularly invited me into classes to help teach and coach younger students. This honoured the years of hard work I'd already put into my creative life and was a huge confidence boost. The solace I'd found in art and music had led me to spend most of my spare time either practicing or creating, and I had naturally become quite skilled, especially relative to my peers.

I also gained a lot of satisfaction from sharing my artistic discoveries with other students, although my being invited to teach and coach was seen as favouritism by some, provoking jealousy and even aggressive behaviour at times. Some of my peers would throw missiles or spit in my direction as I left the art faculty. And this aggressive behaviour wasn't even limited to students. Here's an example, involving a couple of my teachers:

My music teacher, Miss Martin, always related to me as an equal rather than a subordinate, and I'd often swing by her office to chat. She was a kind, generous soul, and always sought to draw the gold out of me. A fine musician in her own right, she respected my burgeoning abilities, and I enjoyed helping in her music classes; I was once even asked to sit in on some practical music examinations to help evaluate the playing standard of the guitarists.

So, within the confines of A Level study, music was actually going okay. But art took a turn for the worse when a new teacher arrived, and, consequently, I was no longer invited to help teach art classes.

One day, after lunch, I headed to the art department early. I liked being there before anyone else so I could work in solitude for a while. My arrival at the art room coincided with Mrs Gilbert's leaving. So, out of courtesy, I asked if it would be okay to make an early start on my work. But no, it wasn't. Mrs Gilbert blustered past, blocking the entrance with her not inconsiderable girth, and promptly locked the door. With arms folded and smug defiance all over her face, she stood like some kind of self-initiated bouncer of the arts, before suggesting that, as an alternative, I should "Go spend time in Miss Martin's orifice, as usual." And, no, that wasn't a spell checker mistake.

To this day, I don't know what Mrs Gilbert had against Miss Martin. It seemed like jealousy. It was certainly disdainful. From different voices, in different places, I was repeatedly met with this kind of treacherously subtle violence against my art and music, and this was far from an isolated incident. To my 17-year-old self, who was simply trying to do good work and keep away from the destructive crowd, these encounters were painfully confusing and yet profoundly shaping in my quest to understand the creative world and my place within it.

SOLACE DENIED

Music was my greatest solace. It was one the place I could run to and escape the turbulence of life.

One day, after somehow surviving another day of school, I came home to find the record player in my bedroom had gone. I never found out where, who took it, or why. I rarely asked such questions.

We weren't an affluent family, so I couldn't afford to buy a new turntable; and besides, I didn't know if that would disappear, too. So, the few vinyls I'd been able to afford with my paltry paper-round money sat on the shelf, in silence, for years.

Even worse than not being able to listen to my favourite music, this also restricted my guitar practice. I desperately wanted to be a professional guitarist and had been working very hard to become a good player by jamming along with the few, precious albums I owned. But all of that ground to a halt.

Whether it was intentional or not, the events in this part of my story sent a clear message to my formative creative heart: my love of music didn't matter, my dreams didn't matter, and my personal peace and place of escape didn't matter either.

It was a numbing experience—a crushing Creative Wound.

There were many other incidents that hammered home a similar message. Not all were huge in their own right, but over time the repetition inflicted a kind of death by a thousand cuts on my creative heart—a slow, lingering, unrelenting ebbing away of my artistic spirit. Here are a few examples:

1. The piano I enjoyed playing at my grandparents' house was unexpectedly replaced with a new sideboard. I remember the devastation when I stepped into the lounge and realised the piano was gone from my life.

2. It was a similar story with an electric organ I used to love, too. During one visit to my grandparents' house, I went to get it from the cupboard, only to discover they'd sold it.

3. Things were no better at school, either. During my middle-school years, such a large proportion of my classmates were so unruly that music lessons were abandoned altogether before I had the chance to play an instrument of any kind—unless you count the time I was custodian of the plastic egg… I'd peer through the window of the locked music cupboard door, shelves stacked with all manner of fantastical instruments, and I'd wonder what it would be like to actually play one. Oh, the fanciful dreams of a child.

4. As a low-income family in a small house, we lived in each other's pockets, and listening to music could easily cause a disturbance. So, to avoid this, I got my first pair of decent headphones. They were my escape, a gateway to solitude and peace. I treasured those headphones, especially as there was no money for replacements. One day a friend came to visit and mistakenly thought my headphones were hinged, and when trying them out they accidentally snapped. My friend, mortified by what he'd done, took them away and promised to see them repaired

or replaced—but I never saw or heard of them again. This was another incident of my creative safe place being stolen from my life, never to return.

Through reading my stories, you can easily pinpoint the areas that mattered most, the predicable ways harm came, and how easy it was for a belief to gain a hold that "This is how things are for me and they will probably never change."

By forensically examining the narratives I've shared, you will have noticed themes and patterns clearly emerge. This reflective approach will work for you and your creative life, too, because the clues to finding your Creative Wound are hidden in your story.

The Clues Hidden In Your Story

Our lives are made up of stories. One by one we gather them. As more time passes, the more stories we own.

What should we make of the times when our creative world was hit with incidences of pain, trauma, neglect or abuse? Surely the best option is to just leave the past in the past and move on, isn't it? Is there really any point investigating the stories that make up our lives?

If your current inclination is to ignore painful incidents and simply try to be positive, I'd like you to consider another approach. Because, by not facing and dealing with incidents of harm in a healthy way, we develop deep-seated subliminal mechanisms to protect ourselves, and over time we stop questioning if they should even be part of us. They just are. And they rarely work in our favour, at least beyond the short-term.

We continually reference our past to frame and inform

our future. So, by engaging healthily with our past, we can keep it in its proper place and be free to launch into a future that is hopeful and new. Therefore, I suggest we be intentional in choosing exactly how the past intersects our present and our future. Leaving it alone is like ignoring a leak in the attic because each drip appears insignificant. For a while you can get away with it, before the whole ceiling eventually comes crashing down.

Not for a moment am I suggesting that navel-gazing, pity parties, or self-indulgence are sensible options. But conversely, neither is numbing-out to cope with a heart-breaking past. Whether we choose passivity or overactivity to shroud ourselves, essential portions of our story remain hidden and unnamed. This could be to hide from the shame we feel when looking them in the eye, or because we consider them inconsequential in nature and we don't want to bother others or disrupt our own lives by going there. But, by refusing to re-enter our backstory, we do ourselves a disservice and our creative heart remains caged.

WHAT ARE YOU ABOUT?

Have you ever considered the possibility that you are a good idea? Not that you are capable of having good ideas, but that you, yourself, *are* a good idea?

You are so much more than just an orderly collection of molecules, and hair, and blood, and bones, and skin. You are a character with a role in the continuing story of the world. This makes you significant.

If you've adopted the notion that you, as a person, are fundamentally a bad idea, it will be difficult to see your work as anything but tainted and unworthy. It's no wonder that attempts to invigorate your creative life are routinely met with frustration. The blockages you experience stem from a deeper place than a lack of inspiration or motivation. They are the embodiment of untrue beliefs.

PAUSE & EFFECT

When a friend tells us of a book she's read, or a film she's just seen, our initial question is nearly always "What is the story about?"

Your creative life is a story. Note I didn't say it was a fairytale or a fantasy. But it is most definitely a story.

Pause to ask yourself: what is your story about? Does your story feel frozen in time?

Imagine you are sitting at home watching a movie with a friend when a phone call arrives for him. So, you hit pause while your friend disappears off into the kitchen to take the call. Meanwhile you wait, patiently staring at the stilled scene on the screen.

For an hour.

A Creative Wound can be like that. You're happily immersed in an engaging, exciting narrative when it is suddenly disrupted and put on hold. Even worse, it seems like you can't restart without permission. You are not the cause of the interruption, but you seem to need the go-ahead from the interrupter to continue—it feels as though you'd be defrauding them to carry on without their green light.

You, my friend, are stuck.

This place of ambivalence is often where we find ourselves in the aftermath of a Creative Wound. Everything freezes. You want to push forward, but you don't. You want to create, but it hurts too much. Sometimes the stuck feeling in the middle of a creative endeavour isn't a lack of ability, ideas or even motivation. It is a Creative Wound.

EPIC OR MUNDANE

You get up, have breakfast, go to work, come home, eat dinner, go to bed. If you're lucky, you might even get a couple of weeks' holiday as a reward for your endurance.

Ad infinitum.

I realise how tempting it is to view life as a banal series of linear events. However, the reality is actually much more interesting, often intriguing, and at times even epic. Yet so many of us are missing it altogether.

Try listening with intent to conversations being had around you. You'll hear people unwittingly reducing their lives to little more than a list of stuff they did and the stuff that happened to them in the gaps between doing the stuff they did.

It may be detailed—descriptive, even—but it is still just a list, nonetheless. There is something profoundly unsatisfying about a conversation made up of detached, episodic facts. And it worsens when the speaker volleys their information bombs at you at incomprehensible speed. It can feel like you've walked on to a quiz show and been caught up in the quick-fire round.

What we need is a return to epic story, and not just on Friday night trips to the cinema, but in how we frame our very existence. Our hearts yearn for the excitement of drama, romance, purpose, and meaning.

By not actively looking to interpret our lives through the lens of story, we resign ourselves to a mundane tally-chart existence—just keep on notching, keep getting things done, as if life were a competition about who can produce the most.

And it's boring.

STORY GIVES CREATIVITY MEANING

Whether we admit it or not, we are engaged in a continual search for meaning, or at least some kind of distraction to dull the ache when we're alone with nothing but our thoughts for company.

No wonder there's such widespread uptake in living vicariously through social media, sports, magazines, and the lives of imaginary people on TV. This has become the primary mental and emotional diet for millions of us. I've found myself here more than once and understand the appeal, especially when feeling weary.

The allure is the call to adventure but without the risk, and an escape from having to admit our life is muted and lifeless. But this is fool's gold. It might glitter and fascinate, but it has little value compared to the real thing. Therefore, we must keep digging because a superficial resemblance to gold is not what we're looking for.

So, why exactly does our creative world feel so dull? What is missing?

PLOT

Plot gives meaning to existence. Plot turns events into a story. And from within story, purpose is unearthed, bringing with it a clearer understanding of the past and a more robust hope for the future. Shifting perspective, to viewing our life as a story, brings a whole new aspect to the monotony of today.

For example, let's take your bank statement. A quick read through it might reveal such ordinary things as:

9 September: takeaway coffee £3

11 September: mobile phone payment £20

13 September: car insurance payment £15

22 September: flowers £25

At first glance, this looks predictably mundane and no different from anybody else's bank statement. But, if we take the time to discover the reasons behind the transactions, even a list of everyday purchases unveils a dramatic story, pregnant with meaning.

Let's take the coffee from 9th September. That was bought while dropping-off your lifelong friend, Rachel, at the airport. She's been offered the job of her dreams, teaching dance at The Juilliard School, and is emigrating to New York. That innocuous-looking £3 transaction is actually laden with incredible sadness for you, and joy for your friend, as the narrative of two lives enters a whole new era of permanent separateness.

Ordinary, mundane events are usually anything but ordinary, mundane events. But you will only ever discover how profoundly they've impacted your creativity if you take the time to investigate the stories of your life.

ASSAULT IN THE AREA OF DESIRE

If you've been hamstrung in a creative area, take it as a sign that this area really matters. For example, the fact my French is appallingly bad doesn't bother me one bit. You can freely insult my *bonjours* all you like and it won't harm me at all. But, if you were to criticise me for sloppy guitar playing, that's a whole other story…

We feel pain the most where it matters the most. Robert Bly, in his book *Iron John,* said it this way, "Where a man's wound is, that is where his genius will be."[1]

This was certainly true for my friend Cam.

Cam works for a high-profile technology blog, producing video reviews watched by millions around the world. He is thankful to be a tech journalist as it was always his dream job. But things could have been very different. Here's what happened to the man whose career depends on being assured and authoritative on camera.

As a 12-year-old, my first history teacher—an old Welsh farmer called (unsurprisingly) Mr. Williams—made us do a news report where we'd write up a quick snippet from history and role-play like we were reporting on modern-day news programmes, in front of a rolling camera. I was so nervous I couldn't speak, and I cried… all of it captured by a camera pointing at my face.

Of course, some kids watched it afterwards and laughed at the fact that I'd cried. High School is mean.

This incident came flooding back to me years later when a work colleague started playing one of my videos out loud during a team meeting. I was immediately filled with embarrassment and asked him to stop. I just couldn't stand it.

The thing is, though, I love making videos. I love the creative process behind every stage. And more importantly, I love kicking my fears and anxieties up the arse. I will not, and cannot, let them control every aspect of my life, and slowly but surely I'm gradually pulling away, one tightly-gripped claw at a time, until one day I barely notice them anymore.

A Creative Wound will always be felt most acutely in the area of our greatest desire. Desire speaks. It is the language of the heart. Desire highlights whatever we consider to be truly significant. By investing the time to write down the stories of your life, and allowing them to be told and retold, themes will emerge. Themes of longing. Themes of decimation. Themes of restoration.

Engage with your own story in an honest, patient and kind manner, and you will find it sheds light on who you are and what your life is about. If you'll commit to this with determined focus, you'll see exactly how and why the Creative Wounds you've received have affected you and your personal expression so much. Armed with this knowledge you'll have a much better chance of healing and minimising any further harm.

How we interpret the recurring themes of our artistic lives affects our responses, which in turn inform our choices, and these ultimately have the biggest influence on the success we have. Exploring our stories will inevitably reveal significant patterns, and so it is vital to discover what these are.

As G.K. Chesterton reminds us "It isn't that they can't see the solution. It is that they can't see the problem."[2]

[PART 3]

HEAL YOUR CREATIVE WOUNDS

Effective ways to revive your artistic soul.

Interpreting Our Stories

Through the careful study of my own Creative Wound stories I noticed particular themes emerge. These themes profoundly shaped my early ideas about the world and enlightened me as to the nature of reality. They influenced my desires, and informed me of the likelihood of these ever being fulfilled.

Whenever you can accurately predict exactly how things are going to go, because you've learned "that's what always happens", you're hitting upon a theme. It may be one of being laughed at every time you present your work to others, or it could be inevitable indifference and silence no matter what you try. Perhaps it seems everybody else gets the breaks and you're always overlooked.

One of my major themes was this: anything enjoyable that connected me to beauty or creativity would inevitably suffer an abrupt end. So I came to believe my artistic expressions were of little-to-no worth, and my aspirations unlikely to receive acknowledgement or nurture. Attempting any form of art was also an open invitation for harm to enter as its compatriot, and what was once a haven of solace now held all the calm of afternoon tea in a hornet's nest.

The risk of pain became so great that I would just keep my work to myself. I didn't share my creative desires often, as presenting them would frequently lead to responses of disinterest, disdain, or even destructiveness. So, I learned to internalise my longings and artistic interests as some kind of protection. At the time, I didn't know what else to do other than aim for survival.

HOW WE NEED OTHERS TO UNDERSTAND OURSELVES

No matter how self-reliant we've allowed ourselves to become, we need other people to help us interpret our world. We need accountants, and lawyers, and doctors, and mechanics, and poets, and scientists, and theologians, and counsellors. We need others to help us make sense of, and give context to, our world so that we can draw informed conclusions about what exactly is going on.

This kind of input is even more necessary in the life of a child because so much is happening for the first time. Often, these experiences repeat throughout the early years without us having the option of choice. This is how our worldview forms.

Children desperately need the intervention of safe, healthy adults, to bring wisdom, clarity, and interpretation to their experiences and feelings. And while I'm not saying you or I were victims of neglect or abuse (although that may be true), it is possible we have grown with a skewed perspective of reality. And as a result, we may have developed a skewed perspective toward our creative hearts.

ENGAGE WITH YOUR OWN STORY

Our brain's ability to interpret and reinterpret events is the secret that makes sharing our stories so transformative. Instead of trying to bury the moments that brought our artistic world such anguish, we can go back—this time taking a friend with us—and reshape how we relate to those events.

If we don't take the time to go back, then we are doomed to filtering our creative lives through the suppressed pain of past harm. Even though many people repeat the adage that time heals all wounds, I don't believe it to be true, at least not in terms of our emotions. Time won't heal your wound. It's what you do with your time that will make the difference.

Whether by choice or not, we've all experienced memories coming back alive in us with the intensity of the day the events happened. If we purposefully revisit and reinterpret our memories then we can reshape them, and their place in our subconscious is robbed of its power to cause us further pain and restriction.

So, how do we do this? By writing, reading, and reinterpreting the stories of harm done to our creative hearts.

By use of intentional reflection we can bring memories back into conscious thought, which makes them malleable, and susceptible to change. This phenomenon is part of the astonishing neuroplasticity of our brains.

WRITE YOUR STORY

Take a look at all that happens in your life with the eye of a storyteller, not an accountant. Take every event out of the mental spreadsheet, placing it into the storybook, and I assure you themes will arise. These themes are clues to who you really are at your core, and will give you tremendous insight into the reason your creativity feels hampered, stuck, or even assaulted.

Story.

Plot.

Themes.

Narrative.

Character.

Reduced by most people to the confines of the glowing screen in the corner of the lounge, these are all powerful tools for unlocking your creative life. This is not a vain search for meaning where there is none but rather an uncovering of foundational truths that lie hidden right in front of your eyes. The narrative of your life hides essential clues to understanding your desires and purpose.

Your real life is where the stories are. Stories are where

the truth of the heart lies, and the truth of your heart is the nucleus of your creativity.

It may be uncomfortable to write details of how your Creative Wounds were sustained if they include the words and actions of others. The important thing to remember is that your stories won't be published, and that naming isn't the same as blaming. To blame someone is to adopt an aggressive, accusatory stance, but in order to write your story you really don't have to take up such a position. Instead, simply detail the incidents that happened, explaining how they affected you, and what your thoughts and emotional responses were. Remember, this isn't a witch-hunt but a process to bring restoration to your creative soul. *However, it is important to write honestly and not diminish the accuracy and intensity of your accounts. If someone acted against you, say it.*

If you have a number of incidents to write about it, you might tackle them at different times so as not to rush or overwhelm yourself. To do this well often requires revisiting the agony of soul that the original incidents caused. So, take your time, and always be kind to yourself as you work.

Grab a pen and paper, sit for a while, and listen to your life.

READ YOUR STORY

The whole idea of stories is that they are meant to be told.

Once we start to see the benefits of documenting our stories, many of us will happily pen them and then hand over the manuscripts for others to read. This can be a deeply transformational act, and yet deeper still remains. This comes by reading our Creative Wound stories aloud to others. It may seem unnecessary, but if you're in the company of one or more people who can hold open a sacred space, then your words and voice will combine in a profound way we seldom get to experience.

This is very different to public speaking or everyday conversation. Your words are not spontaneous but have already been agonised over and purposefully selected. You won't struggle to articulate your thoughts on the spot, or forget an important point, because your thinking has already been done and you're now focused solely on reading. In essence, you are listening to your own words along with whoever else is there with you, and the presence of their witness gives your narrative a new weight and validity.

Every time I've done this, the experience takes my stories to a new place of integration with my current life. The incidents I relay no longer exist in isolation. They escape the confines of my head and gain objective dimensionality because friends are engaging with them, and me, in kindness.

Being heard with empathy and care is an uncommon gift, but offers a way to find out what is holding back our artistic lives. If you've chosen wisely, and have insightful people listening to your story, then be willing to let them reflect back what they hear, and encourage them to offer their own perspectives and interpretation of events as they see them. We are compelled by our lives to make sense of what seems senseless, and becoming a storyteller helps us to do that. By writing and reading our stories we will notice previously unseen angles, patterns, and significances that could prove revelationary and revolutionary if we're willing to embrace the truths they offer.

As Keith R Anderson affirms: "People are changed as their stories are heard."[1]

ILLUMINATION LEADING TO RESOLUTION

Hopefully, by now you can see just how illuminating it can be to engage with our stories. As we gain an understanding of the themes and patterns that emerge, we expose the mindsets and beliefs that govern our relationship with creativity. Many of these are not at all valid, and yet, because of the intense emotion during moments of trauma, our minds and bodies receive them as being beyond question. In fact, if we don't enter these moments again and address them directly, the lies therein will become the very truth that we live by.

It's hard to pinpoint what our limiting beliefs are when we've been living them as the indisputable truth for years. This is why becoming students of our own stories matters so much.

To bring a lasting resolution to our pain, we must start by clarifying our Creative Wounds. As, without knowing what they are and how they happened, we resign ourselves to flailing around in the dark. So, I encourage you to recall and write down your significant stories, then follow all the trails you unearth, with tenacity. Then find the boldness to read your stories aloud to people you trust.

We desperately need the transformation this internal work offers.

Passion & Choice

Have you ever watched those reality TV music competition shows?

The latest fresh-faced wannabe arrives on stage, and under a rainbow of stage lighting, belts out an unintentionally parodied version of a song that was written decades before he was born, by a writer he's never heard of. The song was chosen by the contestant's celebrity coach and has little-to-no connection with the boy singing it; but, he's pretending it does. I bet you can picture him now—hand on heart, face scrunched up in mock sincerity as it competes for attention with his meticulously crafted gravity-defying hair sculpture.

"Such passion!" the celebrity experts cry. Me? I'm not so sure.

If you're anything like me, you might be getting immune to the word *passion*. It is overused, rarely fully understood, and is losing its power. It's going the way of *literally* and *awesome.*

The word *passion* has its origins in the Greek verb *paschó* which means 'to suffer'[1]. The feelings that arise from being impassioned are not just excitement or agitation but are a compelling, intense stirring—a heart-wrenching ache from a bruise deep in the soul. This place is the seat of the world's greatest art, but is far removed from what the TV music competitions deliver. Hype and desperation abound, yes, but not a whole lot of passion. I'll be honest with you, I'm not a fan of the genre. At all.

Ironically, I am regularly contacted by researchers for these shows and have been asked more than once if I would like to compete, or supply artists who've worked with me in the studio. I decline all these requests. Once I was asked to be a judge for a local live singing competition but turned it down. It would have been a great marketing and PR opportunity for myself and the studio, but I noticed myself reacting strongly in opposition to it.

My stance is controversial to some, but elements of these shows seem unavoidably exploitative to me, with the potential to cause a lot of damage to sensitive, creative souls. It doesn't take a psychologist to see that some of the contestants are emotionally vulnerable and in desperate need of affirmation, while others are still in the forma-tive stages of their art. These are people who need help, love, care, and support through mentoring, coaching and counselling. The last thing they need is to be paraded on a stage and judged. In all good conscience, I couldn't bring myself to be part of an event that risked doing that kind of harm to another human being, especially one I had no relationship with. The whole idea was painful, which was when it dawned on me—the pain I felt was pointing to a deeper truth: I was *passionate* about this.

I suspect many of the show contestants struggle after being judged and rejected on national TV. Although, if the pain reveals how intrinsically their art is yoked to their heart, and they can interpret the pain as being a legitimate proof of their passion, then nobody's words—no matter who they are—will be able to shut them down or insist that they stop.

Or start...

At primary school, I joined an after-hours guitar club, where we'd strum and sing simple folk songs, and pop hits from the likes of The Beatles. Somehow I'd caught the ear of the teacher and was singled out for special musical attention. Not that this sensitive, introverted young boy wanted that. I wanted to be invisible, thank you very much.

This is the thing—being judged, even positively, can be damaging if not handled with sensitivity. It's one thing having a gift, but quite another to have the strength of character, temperament, or desire for it to be utilised in the way others think it should be.

CRITIQUE NOT JUDGEMENT

While critique has undeniable value as part of the creative process, you don't have to allow anybody the power to pass permanent judgement over the art that lives in you. Opt out of that game. If your art truly matters to you, then it automatically has value. Period. And if you believe in the message that your work carries, then others will resonate with it too, which is far more important than it having to be perfect. I'm pretty sure neither Bob Dylan nor Bruce Springsteen would ever win one of those televised singing contests, but their work has been loved and appreciated by millions, spanning decades. Wouldn't you rather *that* be your legacy?

Sometimes we feel as though we need permission to create; as if an authority figure has to give us the green light of approval.

So, what do you do if the gatekeepers keep their gates shut to you? What if there's no record deal? What if there's no publisher? What if the self-appointed judges of talent and taste show no interest?

What if that nagging 'lack of consent' feeling is holding you back, but nobody chooses you?

Here's an idea: *you choose you.*

Find Out Who You Are

A pear tree that bears no fruit is no less a pear tree than one that has grown thousands. Any expert's examination of the tree would conclude the same thing. True, it hasn't fulfilled the potential of its existence, but there is no argument about what it actually is, because the tree's identity isn't established by its yield but by what it was made to be. It isn't named and known by its fruit but by its DNA.

This distinction is important.

Similarly, if we were cut to our core, many of us would bleed creativity as our primary identifier. Even if you are yet to produce great work, your DNA still screams "Artist! Creative! Writer! Dancer! Musician!" At an elemental level, you know this is who you are.

To the impatient or uninformed it would be easy to write off a barren tree as being worthless. You might even hack it down and use it as firewood, although this would be a rash move. There are specific conditions that help or hinder the yield of a pear tree and it's not always the lack of potential that holds the tree back. Likewise, it's not always our technical ability that holds us back.

It is often what we believe about ourselves that is our biggest restraint.

And what we believe about ourselves isn't always true.

So, how can we know what *is* true about ourselves unless we accurately know ourselves?

Which prompts the question, how well do we actually know ourselves?

GETTING TO KNOW YOURSELF

How we perceive ourselves and our world hugely impacts our creative output. Yes, it affects the type of work we do, its style, and the techniques we use, but, even more fundamentally, our degree of accurate self-awareness shapes our capacity to create anything in the first place.

The better you understand your wiring, the easier you will discover the lifestyle that best facilitates your flourishing. Without this knowledge, you resign yourself to random experimentation in the hope of stumbling across something that works.

COMPANY CULTURE

My former boss was a pretty good salesman; so the design

agency I was employed by was never short of work, the kind of work I enjoyed. But, curiously, I was miserable there and didn't know why. It was confusing and frustrating. Gamely, I stuck at it, but after a few years it started to erode my enthusiasm and confidence. Almost every client relationship was the antithesis of ease, and as I was the common denominator, I concluded the problem must be me.

I wish I'd known back then what I've since learned about personality types—my frustration and Creative Wounds from that period would have been much less. With the benefit of hindsight, the conflicts I had back then make much more sense today.

As is often the case, my boss's personality profoundly shaped the culture and character of his business. So, working there was a bit like working inside an annexe of his mind; and as he and I didn't always agree, or particularly enjoy each other's company, this was a big reason I never felt at home in that job. Furthermore, he tended to attract clients who gelled well with him, which conversely meant they were often people I struggled to click with.

An intriguing thing I've discovered since starting my own business in 2005 is that the same principle of attraction that worked for my former employer began working for me, too. Many of my current clients have become good friends and we've enjoyed delightful working relationships for years.

This highlights the impact that personality has on our

creative lives, and how understanding each other's personalities enables us to respond with empathy and wisdom,
not least when one of us is experiencing conflict, pain,
or confusion.

We're not always quick to consider alternative perspectives, but it's a big mistake to believe our way of thinking
is the only way to think.

IT'S MY PARTY

The lens of personality we each view the world through
affects our responses in wildly different ways.

For example, we all have friends who would feel loved
beyond measure if we were to throw them a surprise
party; they would come alive while being engulfed by
a roomful of unexpected guests, revelling for hours in
blissful celebration. However, if you did that for me, I'd
thank you for the sentiment, wish everyone an enjoyable
evening, and then promptly leave.

PERSONALITY ASSESSMENT TESTS

I have tried a number of different personality analysis tools,
and there is a great deal of insight to be gained from them
all. Overall, I've resonated most with The Myers Briggs
Type Indicator and The Enneagram (which I've found it
to be very fluid, bending along with our natural human
shifts in mood and state).

However, my point here isn't to advocate one method
over another, but instead to encourage you to at least

dip your toe into the water and experience some of the revelationary benefits available.

If you haven't given much time to personality assessment tools before, you may be surprised at how quickly you can improve your understanding of both yourself and others. While it's possible to take this kind of study to very deep levels, making a solid start doesn't have to be difficult, expensive or time-consuming. You can even begin your journey by completing simple tests online. While these can sometimes lack robustness, they are usefully indicative and provide a strong launch point at no cost.

LIMITING YOUR VULNERABILITY TO CREATIVE WOUNDS

Let's be honest, most of us are interested in our own personality type more than anybody else's, at least at first. And it is vital to understand ourselves as fully as we can. But, once we've got a good handle on that, the real fun starts in learning about people who are not like us, and how we fit into the bigger picture. This helps us establish a grounded sense of place and belonging.

Once we understand other people's frameworks for thinking, feeling, and acting, our personal susceptibility to Creative Wounds is dramatically reduced.

Here's an example why:

Jon has been working on songs for his new album. He's tentatively excited about the whole thing and would love to hear the thoughts of a trusted friend about the direction he is heading. So, he creates some MP3 audio files from the recordings-in-progress and emails them to his friend Kelly to find out her thoughts.

Unfortunately, what Kelly replies with is quite crushing. In her best attempts to be helpful, she picks apart every detail: recording quality, choice of instruments, a guitar that is a hair out of tune, subtle inflections in Jon's singing that could be improved. She sends back quite a list.

Kelly's idea of giving feedback for a work-in-progress was to pinpoint all the areas of weakness so they didn't ruin the final work—which was a long way from what Jon needed. By asking for comments on a work-in-progress, he was looking for thoughts and affirmations on his broader concepts and general direction—the big picture, visionary stuff. He needed this to help bolster his belief in the project so that he had the impetus to keep working, safe in the knowledge that it had potential and was heading somewhere good.

So, who was right and wrong? Neither person. This encounter demonstrates that, through the filter of personality type, Jon and Kelly had radically different understandings of what the interaction was intended to achieve.

Kelly is an Enneagram Type One—typically quite perfectionistic and thus quick to spot all the faults in a piece of work. So, it is an act of kindness for her to highlight all the defects she sees, knowing this will help Jon perfect his work. However, Jon is Enneagram Type Four—a creative, emotional and tender soul. So, at this stage of his creative process, feedback such as Kelly offered can unintentionally bring with it discouragement and deflation, as Jon's desire was for someone else to see the big picture alongside him, and affirm his pursuit of the whole project in the first place.

It is clear to see the level of misunderstanding possible from what seems like a straightforward interaction between friends. Thankfully, the more time we invest in understanding our own paradigms and how they differ from others, the better we can interpret and comprehend one another.

Armed with this knowledge, it is easy to recognise that Kelly would be an amazing asset to Jon as his project approached its conclusion. This is the time when feedback from a perfectionist personality is your best friend—they will catch any major problems before they become permanent.

KNOW YOURSELF TO UNDERSTAND OTHERS

As you better recognise and understand your own thinking style, you'll naturally start to trust yourself and your decisions more. Plus, being aware of your weak spots is crucial when choosing friends who have complementary strengths—friends who can offer insight into areas you may overlook on your own.

In relation to my own work, I greatly value constructive comments from my creative friends. However, I do consider which personality type I am sharing with. I also take into account the stage of the process I am in and the type of feedback that will be most constructive at that particular point. Doing this has helped reduce the amount of accidental Creative Wounds I've suffered. Plus, my friends feel more valued, as they're asked to contribute in their particular area of strength and are free to speak honestly. Everybody wins.

DO UNTO OTHERS?

There is a popular belief that you ought always to treat people how you'd wish to be treated yourself. But, in light of how radically different our personalities can be, I'd suggest that—beyond common decency—we should instead seek to treat people how *they'd* prefer to be treated. This is why my personal mission is to better understand people and the reason for their actions.

As members of the creative nation, we can be particularly susceptible to criticism, so the next time you're asked for feedback on someone's work, why not ask them what kind of feedback they'd like? Your courtesy and sensitivity is sure to be appreciated, and you're much more likely to respond with genuinely useful comments.

Isn't it time you became better acquainted with yourself?

Good Ground

We all know people who 'could have been' a rock star, a professional footballer, or whatever esteemed profession you choose. You'll also find those in every field who are famous for never making it, a curious notoriety that must really sting. The truth is, it's not always ability that holds us back but the conditions in which we are trying to be fruitful.

You've felt it. This sense of resistance to your success. It can be palpable, but not straightforward to diagnose. Complex, uncontrollable factors conspire to frustrate your best efforts and extinguish your creative hopes.

The easy route is to examine your body of work, find it lacking in quality or quantity (usually both), and sink into crippling self-doubt. This may be how you feel about yourself and your art. If so, are you treating yourself fairly?

Possibly not.

WHY CONDITIONS MATTER

Let's return to our earlier pear tree analogy and dig a little deeper.

To grow well, a pear tree needs to be planted in good soil with exposure to sunlight. The nutrients supplied by these base elements are essential for proper growth and productivity. You can, of course, choose to plant a tree in a darkened corner and feed its roots with depleted, low-grade soil. But, realistically, you can't expect a great harvest as the tree has little to work with. Its fruitlessness isn't due to lack of potential but rather its sub-optimal environment.

Within our creative lives, we must intentionally feed on nutrients that enrich and nourish our souls. These vary person-by-person, but by paying attention to the fundamentals, we will make marked improvements to our creative conditions. And when the time comes to get our hands dirty and create, we will fare much better when our environment is no longer working against us.

So which specific conditions you should look at?

THE LOCATION FOR CREATION

I used to work for a design agency in a UK city that regularly topped the 'worst place to live' charts.

Our office was part of a drab industrial estate on the rough side of town. The building—a cheap post-war prefabricated box made of dull grey metal panels—perfectly complemented the swathes of tedium that sprawled around us on all sides. As I gazed out of my office window, I could see for inches.

Daily for three years I would drive an hour to the office and, whether I felt like it or not, produce creative work on demand. During this time I learned to dig deep and see beyond the physical space I was occupying in order to access the inspiration I needed. Despite the glamorous public visage, this is often what the life of a creative professional actually looks like.

Decision.

Craft.

Grind.

Creating beauty on time and on budget. Day after day.

Truthfully, the draining effect of this environment was a massive reason I left to start my own business. If you, too, conclude that your environment is hindering you from being your creative best, then why not consider moving somewhere different? This might be as simple as writing your book from an alternate coffee shop, as radical as retraining for a completely new career, or as drastic as moving your whole life to a different part of the world.

The profound effect that conditions play in human development have been well documented. You may recall the infamous orphanages discovered in communist Romania during the 1980s. These cruelly restrictive environments had a devastating impact on the development of tens of thousands of lives—evidence that so many children's failure to thrive had little to do with their potential and everything to do with the conditions they found themselves in.

The effects have been long lasting, too. Over thirty years later, many of the survivors are still without homes or family, and live among the rats in the filth of Bucharest's underground sewers.[1]

Of course, this is an extreme example, but suitably shows how environment can inhibit our ability to thrive. Over time, restrictive conditions can warp our thinking and skew our perspective on our place in the world.

If you suspect conditions are squashing your creativity, investigate further. This may be significant. Just because others are in the same position doesn't advocate its goodness or suitability for your life.

I appreciate that radical change isn't always possible overnight, and it's not always practical to relocate from where you live and work, especially if you have friends, family or other responsibilities there. But if your current location drags you down then answer honestly: what is stopping you exploring new possibilities? Who says you have to stay there long term?

A RESERVOIR OF RECOLLECTIONS

What if you could experience more inspiration than you currently do? How would that improve your creative life?

Even though the most fulfilling option is, undoubtedly, to find a physical place that fuels your imagination and ignites your enthusiasm, perhaps relocating is impossible, or is at least a slower process than you'd like. Don't lose heart, good news exists. There is a way to experience the positive emotions of your favourite places without even being there—by intentionally using memories.

All of us carry memories. We can't help it. So, why not create and use them on purpose?

To do this, it is important is to build up a reservoir of recollections—positive memories of the places you love. The trick is to commit moments to memory while they are happening, perhaps capturing images with a camera, or taking small physical reminders away with you where possible to aid your recollection. This process is like charging up your internal battery with memories of good feelings. Afterward, when you bring back to mind the memories of these places or experiences, you can draw upon the energy you stored-up, and power yourself through the less-than-ideal times.

Changes in our brain chemistry alter our emotions, and we can bring these changes about on purpose using our thoughts. This technique intentionally focuses the mind on good memories associated with that particular place we'd rather be. Every day, millions of people change their brain chemistry to alter their feelings by drinking copious amounts of alcohol. Or perhaps they take drugs, or bungee jump from silly heights. But I believe there is a better, healthier, way for us creatives to make use of this gift inside our heads.

Here's an example:

As day breaks, I often step outside into our garden and look up, staring deep into that one big sky that connects us all. This morning it was bright blue, with piercing sunshine a foreshadow of the approaching springtime. I stood and stared upward, soaking in the vastness of it all.

These few moments helped me tap into wonderful recollections of times under blue Australian skies with my wife, Sarah, reawakening memories of the people, culture and land I found myself pining for. And, although I couldn't be back there right then, I could draw from the well of happy memories I held inside, and experience again the inspired feelings I enjoyed while we were there. So, even though I wasn't physically in Australia, I could experience something of Australia coming alive inside of me. This helped put my mind and emotions in a more conducive state. I relaxed, and creativity was able to flow much more readily.

THINKING ON PURPOSE

In Greek mythology, the nine daughters of the god Zeus were said to be the supernatural embodiment of the arts, known as the Muses. Today, a muse is something or someone who gives impetus to our artistic work. As creative people, it can be as though we are always chasing an encounter with one of these muses in search of a frustratingly elusive moment of inspiration.

Our language today informs us of their influence on the mindset of artists, writers and performers. For instance, we visit museums, we play music, and are amused by comedy. You may have even mused over the points I've just made.

However, the state of flow and inspiration we crave is less likely to be a visitation from a Greek God and more about creating optimal states for our minds to function at their best.

In light of this, the concept of thinking on purpose as a transformational tool for our emotions is revolutionary, given that our emotions play such a large part in how motivated or inspired we feel. So, don't wait days or weeks for inspiration to turn up—go and track it down. It is hidden in plain sight, camouflaged against the memories of a significant place and time. Ruminate on these memories and they'll breathe new life into you, with pleasant creative emotions soon to follow.

So, stop blaming the mythical muse's lack of personal attentiveness for your artistic malaise. Using memories on purpose is a better alternative to just sitting around waiting for spontaneous motivation to hit you.

Memories are an essential part of our creative arsenal. They're far more than just a record of events, so fashion them with intentionality. Create the specific memories you want to have. Design them. Then, when everything in your environment screams in opposition to creative fertility, unleash these memories to ignite your inspiration.

Inspiration

Some of our best creative moments arrive in the twilight between consciousness and unconsciousness. When fully awake, our brains emit beta waves, but when relaxed, the waves change to alpha—sometimes referred to as being 'in alpha state'.

You'll recognise the feeling: finding yourself 'miles away' while driving on an endless, straight road. Or being lost in thought during a hot shower. I don't know how many times Sarah asks why I've spent so long in the bathroom on a morning. Time loses its consistent, predictable rhythm and we slip into an eternal space. Thoughts drift, swirl, and swim. It feels like five minutes, but it's closer to twenty.

This is 'being in the zone'. Or 'in a state of flow'. It's when the sense of self melts into the background, and you feel much more alive to the focus of your creativity.

Simply put, it's daydreaming on purpose. Babies and toddlers spend a lot of time in this realm, soaking up experiences in their subconscious mind, and then re-presenting their findings in new, creative ways.

GIVE YOUR CREATIVE BRAIN SOME SPACE

Because of my constant desire to learn and grow, coupled with a busy life, I got myself into a place where I would cram audiobooks and podcasts into every crack of time I could. The part of my mind that loves the rational and logical, and has a continual thirst for wisdom and knowledge, thrives on this. So, whenever I'd take my daughter out in the pram to walk her to sleep I'd have earphones in, and someone with interesting things to say would accompany every drive in the car.

But in doing this I'd actually been overwhelming myself and had not allowed my soul adequate room to breathe. Trying to be creative by relying entirely on the rational brain is severely limiting because the intuitive part of our mind, which lives in the subconscious, is the key to unlocking inspiration and imagination.

Our subconscious is the genius part that recognises patterns, makes connections, and presents concepts we'd never thought of before. You know things you don't know you know; and this is where they live. But in order to hear our subconscious, we need stillness and space to allow it to speak. We've become so attuned to the many voices shouting for our attention that we have lost the art of listening to ourselves.

So, why not:

Turn off the TV. Just sit and stare instead.

Allow yourself to drive in silence.

Unplug your earphones.

Your creative genius exists just below the grasp of conscious thought. It is lurking in the emotional and intuitive parts. As it doesn't live in the rational places, you could even consider it as living in the irrational part of your mind. There's something of a stigma attached to the use of the word irrational as being undesirably out of control, or even lacking intelligence, but here we can embrace its healthy side and give it the credence and respect it deserves.

Over the years, many people have said I'm naturally more creative than they are. But, honestly, I'm not convinced that is entirely true. I probably just discover more in this particular area because I spend comparatively less time focused on the sensory world, and more time engaging my intuitive introverted parts. It is very expansive down here!

In the sensory world, we exist within its imposed limitations, but within our minds whole other universes can exist; and if we don't give ourselves the freedom to explore, we'll never, ever find them. Think, for a moment, of the enormity of the worlds brought to life inside author J. R. R. Tolkien's soul, which birthed epic books such as *Lord Of The Rings* and *The Silmarillion*; or C. S. Lewis and the seven-book *Chronicles Of Narnia*. These writings have delivered a richness and delight to our world, thrilling readers and inspiring authors for decades. These writers knew a lot about trawling the depths of their intuitive imagination and netting the treasures they discovered there.

Of course, logic and language were also necessary to capture and convey the thoughts, emotions, narratives, and characters that came to life inside them, but this secondary part always follows the initial spark of inspiration and internal picture or feelings. This most wild and organic part of the creative act can be exhilarating, and clearly distinguishes the truly inspired from the formulaic and algorithmic.

So, how exactly do we tune into this place of subconscious flow to find better ideas, and ignite our creative flame?

TUNING INTO THE FLOW

Let's be honest, experiencing irrational thoughts and feelings can make you feel vulnerable. It's easy to be judged, or at least to feel judged. Even by yourself.

So, the first step is to create a safe place for your personal creative flow to happen.

When a new idea emerges it can be like looking at one of those magic eye pictures. You must look through it to see it. So, soften your mental focus to being more dream-like, while at the same time not losing your gaze, and then capture something of the essence there before you lose sight by blinking or looking away.

Due to the delicate, ethereal nature of an emerging idea, I don't recommend immediately sharing what you see with unsupportive or intuitively blind people. Critical comments at this stage rarely give the idea an improved chance of survival. So, when your newborn idea arrives, simply observe it and don't critique. Acknowledge its presence, yes, but don't judge what it is or what it may mean. Just take note of it.

It brings to mind how a newborn baby is unable to see clearly. When my daughter and I first looked into each other's eyes, her world was far more blurred than mine. To her, my head looked like an amorphous blob. But over time, that amorphous blob became ever clearer, until at last she could see my egg-like head in all its splendour. This may explain why, one morning after gently brushing Mummy's hair with a soft hair brush, she then did mine with a spoon.

Anyway, I digress.

Here's my advice, contrary to the school-day rebukes that shamed you into abandoning your vibrant imagination: let your mind drift. Daydream.

If you're finding that difficult, then it may be worth first giving your mind something to ruminate on in order to start things off.

PRIME THE PUMP

Back when farms still depended on hand-pumped water

drawn from wells, pumps were fed with a little water to create sufficient suction for the water to be drawn from deep beneath the ground. This is called priming the pump.

In the same way, whenever starting any creative work, I recommend that you first 'prime the pump'. To do this you could:

Pull one of your favourite books from the shelf and read a few pages of quality writing.

Gaze upon some of your favourite paintings, photography, architecture.

Close your eyes and listen to music that reaches down deep and profoundly moves your heart.

You get the idea. It's not overly complex, but it is important. Feed yourself a little of what you want to draw out. Expose yourself to art and creativity that inspires you. Even art of genres you're not actively involved with can be intriguing and lead to moments of innovative synthesis.

So, if you feel blank when daydreaming, first, prime your pump.

MUSIC AND YOUR MIND

I find that listening to music I love also helps put me into a state conducive to creative work, whether the work is directly music related or not.

Music is a language of the subconscious. It has the power to bypass the conscious, analytical mind and agitate the soul.

There is even music available specifically designed to enhance alpha brainwave activity. Personally, I struggle to listen to these scientifically crafted sounds even though they are designed to help with concentration or meditation. For some reason they irritate me as opposed to tuning me in. However, I have discovered that as I've been writing, this book has developed its own soundtrack. And, instead of calm, meditative music, it has been complex and energetic music that has drawn the best out of me. Steve Vai's landmark album, *Passion And Warfare*, has featured prominently.

My theory is that due to me being a chiefly internal person (The Myers-Briggs Type Indicator casts my personality as INFJ) the music's high energy stimulation draws me up to the surface of the sensory world. Sometimes I need a 'fishing hook' to drop, attach to something deep inside me, and then draw up whatever it finds there.

My overarching point here is to encourage you to experiment with a variety of music or alpha-wave soundscapes, and see how each impacts your creativity. I know there are benefits to be had, although they're perhaps not as predictable and cookie-cutter as some studies might suggest.

The brain and music are incredibly complex in their interaction with each other, and the outcomes truly fascinating. Take synaesthesia, for example, where the senses become confused or cross-stimulated. This is something I experience. On hearing certain sounds, my brain can interpret them as colours, or shapes. I imagine that this is where phrases like an angry person 'seeing red' come from.

Curiously, I also see the days of the week as colours. One day, I asked my mum if she'd ever experienced the same phenomena. We'd never discussed this before, and were amazed to discover that not only did she also perceive the days of the week as colours, every one of the seven days was identical to mine!

While synaesthesia is no doubt entertaining, it can some-times make communicating ideas a challenge. Only this morning I tried to describe a vocalist's vibrato as being shaped like "…the undulations of a row of mashed potato scoops from a mashed potato scooper." I suspect they don't teach this kind of thing at the Royal Academy Of Music.

So, take my cue and don't be afraid to be a bit weird. Don't demand instant perfection from yourself as you'll damage yourself trying. And you really don't need to be perfect. Relax. Flow. Create. See what comes. You can edit later. Your physical body demonstrates how to do this. It maintains itself by separating the good stuff from waste material. And we don't stop eating food because it isn't 100 percent perfect nutrition, do we? Approach your work in the same way.

Create, edit, and then discard.

Community

I catch myself releasing an involuntary, contented sigh after typing these two short sentences: "I see you. I hear you." Just the thought of it. The anticipation. The realisation it actually is a possibility. This in itself settles me.

To be heard is to come home. When an individual slows in order to listen to another, they offer a gift of great magnitude. This gift bears witness to the speaker's worthiness, their value. If you adopt a ferocious silence and attend to every one of my words, you honour me. When your questions arise from a place of curiosity, then I am truly received.

However, spending time to *truly* listen to one other can be rare. So, out of necessity, our personal creativity can take on greater responsibility for our wellbeing. As a major artery into our deep heart, it can seem the truest way to connect ourselves to the rest of humanity.

But this carries with it a tension; especially when the prevailing message to our hearts is that we're simply not enough in ourselves to warrant being engaged with beyond the immediacy of surface-level chatter. We're not attractive enough. Not funny enough. Not intelligent, confident, or useful enough. Not rich or popular enough.

On the other hand, if we were to disclose everything we held inside, it would be too much for many. The depth of questioning. The desires, and longings. The pains, cravings, and shame. They say we're too intense. Too complex. Too overwhelming.

It's hard, isn't it? Being too much *and* not enough, both at the same time.

So, where do we turn?

Art.

We create.

We send our work out ahead of us—an envoy, commissioned as both a herald and a bridge of connection with others, in the anticipation that we will somehow be seen, heard, and understood. This is vital when our lives are being interpreted by others as thriving and that we have no obvious needs, yet, beneath our calm visage, we are screaming for a place of belonging that few have the awareness to recognise. Or, if they do notice, they don't know how to acknowledge it and respond. So, in defiance of our true self's invisibility, we send up the beacon of our creative work in the hope of attracting help.

Even though our art isn't literally us, it does represent all that we are. Our work is an ambassador sent in our stead:

Do you see me? Can you hear me? I'm adrift. I want to mat-ter to someone as much as others matter to me. Here are my deepest recesses laid bare on canvas, or in a song, a poem. Does anybody see them? Can anybody interpret what they see? Will anyone come looking—for me?

But, even if nobody responds, we are still not alone. You see, the canvas hears us. It listens with utmost patience as, without judgement, our emotions are absorbed into the paint and then released with every stroke of the brush. And, in doing so, somehow we are less alone.

FLESH AND BLOOD, AND WIRE AND WOOD

It may sound weird, but my guitar is one of my best con-fidants. My feelings toward it are like those for a good friend. Without fail, every encounter between us draws a response. As I drag my fingers across six phosphor-bronze lengths of wire stretched over a hollow wooden body, music blooms and fills the room. Vibrations resonate within the depths of my chest. The strings I choose are heavier than average, but I like the resistance. The push-back makes me dig deep and find another strength, and I'm gratified by the more forceful tone. There's even a risk of danger present: the lack of give in heavy strings means that a misdirected stroke has the potential to draw blood—which it sometimes does. But the appeal here is not self-flagellation; it is confirmation of being alive and present. This is a transfer of emotional energy in a back-and-forth dialogue, the kind my deep heart craves for, and it truly is quickening; a vital exchange between flesh and blood, and wire and wood.

I can play my guitar alone for hours and never once feel lonely.

MISDIRECTED SUPPORT

I have been a fan of Hull City football club since 1984 when my dad took me to my first game. Since then, hundreds of times, I've sat in the hallowed stands of Boothferry Park, and subsequently the KCom Stadium, to support my team; and over the years I've grown to understand a lot about the dynamics and behaviour of a football crowd. But, on Tuesday, September 30, 2003, I witnessed something completely new. Something which deepened my understanding of how to interpret people and the support they offer.

The occasion was Hull City v Swansea City in the English Second Division. In a turn of good fortune I had managed to get hold of four complimentary tickets, so on this chilly autumn evening I took three friends along to watch the game. As we took our seats, I gazed around the stadium. The 21,000 people there filled it almost to capacity, and the atmosphere intensified with anticipation as kick-off approached. Hull City were having one of their best seasons in decades and there was a real excitement about the place, and this particular game mattered a lot. If they could beat Swansea, Hull would register their third consecutive win and go to the top of the table.

Even though I'm a veteran of hundreds of matches, this one stands out in my memory. We were an interesting bunch: three of us friends were long-term football fans, while the other one had never watched a game before in his life. To be fair, Dave had no real interest in sport but had gamely tagged along for the experience, which characterised his wonderfully curious attitude. So, in the sporting spirit, I explained to him the background and context to the game as best I could, sincerely hoping my friend would enjoy the drama and be caught up in the immediacy of a live contest.

As the match progressed, two key incidents arrested my attention. They weren't about the game as such. They were about Dave. In the first one, Lee Trundle, Swansea's star player, broke through Hull's defence and unleashed a shot on goal. Thankfully the shot was tame, and the ball trickled harmlessly into the welcoming gloves of Hull's goalkeeper. Suddenly, Dave leapt to his feet, clapping furiously while everyone close by turned to see who was applauding, and—more importantly—why! That shot on goal was such a non-event that even the Swansea fans weren't applauding the attempt, and nor were the Hull fans clapping their goalkeeper's 'save'. But Dave had seen something that excited him, and so off he sprung, express-ing his appreciation. All by himself.

The second incident came when, after 27 minutes had elapsed, Hull City scored what turned out to be the only goal of the game—the apex of an hour-and-a-half of intense group agony. The blessed relief was palpable as Hull's Stuart Elliott headed the ball into the back of the Swansea net—cue thousands of men, women, boys and girls jumping to their feet to release a deafening roar of celebration. Dave? Dave just sat there.

I've pondered this game, and these incidents, many times over the years. What were Dave's experiences of that game, and just how differently were he and I interpreting the same events? More importantly, what has this got to do with people supporting us and our work?

SURROUND YOURSELF WITH CHEERLEADERS

I encourage my clients to surround themselves with cheerleaders as much as possible. I don't mean pom-pom-waving dancers, but enthusiastic, vocal supporters—people who believe in you and what you do. Everyone I consider to be a friend is also a cheerleader of some kind. And, in return, I do my best to support and spur my friends on with their work.

One lesson I learned from watching Dave at the football was that, even with the best of intentions, cheerleaders can't cheer effectively if they don't have an interest in the game, or haven't had adequate enough exposure to understand its rules. Nor can they respond and encourage appropriately if they haven't grasped the aims of whoever it is they are trying to support.

This is why a clear understanding of what you do, and why, is vital for anyone you allow to deeply influence your creativity. If you are not accurately heard, and fully understood, even the most genuine attempts at encouragement can seem like insincere platitudes, or even random acts of bizarreness. And it's even more awkward when the cheerleader doesn't realise their own lack of experience is showing.

The fast pace of an unfamiliar sport was too much for Dave to comprehend at the first time of asking (Which is entirely understandable, I'd be exactly the same if you took me to a game of Aussie Rules Football.) The nuance and strategy that makes the game so enthralling for many of us were, to him, lost in a blur of noise, colour and movement. So, the simple, pedestrian passage of play he applauded so vigorously revealed his naturally embryonic understanding. His cheering was genuine alright—clearly heartfelt, but due to his limited experience and insight, the only person it benefited was himself. It offered no *actual* support to the team, although it did wonders to invigorate the cheerer himself—who was, it has to be said, having a whale of a time.

This kind of interaction is worth keeping a keen eye out for, as it can be confusing or upsetting for a cheerleader when your response to their most genuine attempts to encourage you is, at best, muted, and often one of bafflement or even hurt. So, try to be kind whenever it happens to you, and seek to understand the motivation and perspective of the cheerleader if you can—as it's likely they haven't fully understood yours.

This lack of comprehension also inhibits the cheerleader from being able to celebrate your victories. While watching the match, Dave was so far behind the pace he hadn't anticipated the possibility of a goal as it approached, nor was he able to respond, even when over 20,000 other people were on their feet cheering. He just didn't get it.

At one point he was the only one standing, and at another point he was the only one sitting—his responses perfectly reversed. If you have cheerleaders who are blind to your desires and unaware of the parameters you're working within, it is likely you will receive this inverted kind of support. It has an uncanny ability to consistently miss the point, and neither cheerleader nor artist connect in what ought to be a fulfilling shared experience. In fact, this kind of interplay can create a painful relational gulf that generates an unpleasant aftertaste of frustration and misunderstanding. It is difficult for everyone when a cheerleader offers you the best they have and yet their support seems disingenuous and hollow.

So, surround yourself with people who understand you and show a willingness to learn the nuances that characterise your creative world. And, on your part, take responsibility to educate those who wish to offer support. Don't presume that things are obvious, and do be patient. Otherwise, you risk having nothing in common with each other, and your cheerleader won't be able to remind you that you have what it takes, because they'll never actually know if you do.

GATHER YOUR OWN TRIBE

In *The INFJ Writer* by Lauren Sapala, she tells the story of how she set up a writing group in Seattle inspired by the Alcoholics Anonymous model. The group would meet together once a week and sit for an hour in a coffee shop to write. No judgement. No critique. No distraction. No fear. They would just sit and write.

This kind of fellowship brings a certain camaraderie and strength you don't know is missing until you experience it. Unlike working in a more academic setting, where criticism and grades and awards and funding all play a part in influencing the purity of the advice, guidance, and attention you may receive, this model works as unadulterated moral support. The presence of one or more people cutting the same path as you is enough to instil new courage. And it is courage that we all need when recovering from Creative Wounds: a heart fellowship over the mutual love of our soul's deep passion.

Even though our creative work often takes place in isolation, having a settled sense of connectedness and a valid place of belonging makes a big difference to the quality of our work and, more importantly, to our overall health as individuals.

The more unique and esoteric our work is, the more isolated it can make us feel. So, consider using the connecting power of the internet, and hunt for other people around the world who share your passion. I guarantee they are out there. You may discover that a group already meets in an area close by, or you could gather people and create your own tribe. You don't have to find 10 other people to start, either. Just two of you is enough to break the isolation and start gaining strength from one another.

THE ROLE OF COMMUNITY IN HEALING

If you're anything like me, you probably enjoy having lots of alone time to think, feel, and create. However, especially if you're healing from a Creative Wound, then the support of other people is a vital component in the mix of your restoration. This wasn't a particularly welcome truth to me on my own journey as it seemed much easier to keep people at a distance in order to minimise any future harm. But, it is very hard to heal completely while you're isolated. People are usually involved in our biggest wounds and therefore it takes relationships to see us fully restored.

Healing is labour. A labour of love; not least love for ourselves. And it takes real courage. To pick up a pencil once more, or to dance after years of crippling self-doubt; that is an act of bravery. And we need people to witness our wound and the bravery of our reawakening. By bringing our story, soul desires, and heroic movements toward wholeness into the presence of safe, trusted friends, suddenly our strength is multiplied as our tribe of allies shares the weight we've carried alone for far too long.

Allow me to share the story of one my musical heroes.

JASON BECKER—GUITAR GENIUS

When I was a teenager first learning guitar, Jason Becker was one player I aspired to be like. I'd faithfully buy the USA-import magazine *Guitar Player* for his regular tutorial column, and his virtuosic instrumental albums were always spinning on my record player.

This man has been an inspiration to me since 1986, back then because of his talent, but now more so because of his heart.

At the age of 20 he joined David Lee Roth's band to work on Roth's album *A Little Ain't Enough*, replacing the venerated Steve Vai. It looked as though this young musician's career was about to go stratospheric. But, tragically, Becker's performing career was cut short by Amyotrophic Lateral Sclerosis (ALS), the same condition Professor Stephen Hawking famously suffered with. In 1996, Becker lost the ability to speak, and he now communicates with his eyes using a system developed by his father. But despite his restriction, Jason continues composing new music using a computer.

Did you catch that? Over 20 years later, Jason Becker is still composing music, and the only things he can move are his eyes!

NOT DEAD YET

In 2012 a movie was made about his life so far, called *Not Dead Yet*, and I'm not ashamed to let you know it reduced me to a blubbering wreck. It also served to strengthen my resolve to make the best music I can and help as many other people as possible realise their particular artistic dreams.

THE NEW ALBUM

Nobody would have blamed Jason if he threw in the towel on music, and indeed life, but he has done anything but. And on December 7th 2018 Jason Becker put out a new solo album, *Triumphant Hearts*, with the help of a bunch of famous friends and crowdfunding support from fans.

Guest performers on the project include such guitar luminaries as Steve Vai, Joe Satriani, Joe Bonamassa, Paul Gilbert, Marty Friedman, Michael Lee Firkins, Neal Schon and Richie Kotzen—to name just a handful of the many who've lent their talents to Becker's new compositions.

I don't know about you, but I can't help but be inspired by a man who won't let what seems like a cruel robbery of immense talent steal his spirit, or steal his music.

I know Jason's new album doesn't feature his fingers on the strings anymore, but his spirit still permeates the music, and that's what truly counts. This is a beautiful example of what it means to call on a tribe of friends to help carry you and your art to a place you can't reach alone. There's no shame in getting the help you need so that your art comes to life. It's a heroic move.

So, in those inevitable moments when you feel hopeless

and crushingly limited, ask yourself the question: *what would Jason do?*

Forgiveness

One of the most thorny, oft evaded, and frequently mis-understood subjects is that of forgiveness. It may seem an obscure theme in relation to producing your best work, but as our truest creativity comes from the heart, a sick heart will only allow work that's in some way inhibited by malady. So we owe it to ourselves to look at the condition of this part of our interior world.

As many a tortured artist will attest, expressing intense pain through creativity can be wonderfully cathartic. Goodness knows, I've done enough of it myself and found it to be potent therapy. However, few of the songs I've written in these moments have been heard by anybody but me. They served a wonderful purpose at the time but are of little real worth to anybody else. Many people have asked if I am wasting decent songs by keeping them to myself, and yes, it can seem that way at times. But I question the notion that the highest and best we can hope to achieve with our creativity is that of a dumping ground for our emotional waste. Are the people who engage with our art not worth more than that?

Are we ourselves not worth more than that?

HEALING YOUR BROKEN ART

Beyond using art as an element toward healing and wholeness, I advocate that we approach ourselves and our creativity in a more holistic way. Let's dare to go deeper, bravely exploring realities that far exceed our emotional condition's limitations. True, many artists rely a great deal on their feelings and consider them the only true source of inspiration for authentic creativity, but this is like claiming the best driving experience is in a vehicle careering wildly out of control. Just as a skilled driver regains control of a skidding car, we can harness the power and intensity of our emotions with devastatingly creative effect if we grasp the wheel of our feelings with fierce intentionality, and purposefully direct our momentum. Emotions are a powerful asset under the bonnet but can be disastrous in charge of the wheel.

REACH THE PINNACLE OF YOUR POTENTIAL

Great art connects communities with epic tales of shared experiences. Great art stands for something. It also stands against something. Great art explores different vectors of the human condition and the world we inhabit. Great art is beautiful. It can be both refined and raw as it encourages the search for truth in its most elemental form. So, in light of this, to reach the pinnacle of your potential you must go beyond having one single perspective. If you find your creative work emanates from the same wounded source every time you write, paint or perform, then perhaps parts of your heart aren't as whole as they might otherwise be. So, if you've suffered a Creative Wound and the pain of it won't leave you, then consider incorporating intentional acts of forgiveness into your creative life. If you don't, the person or incident at the root of your suffering will ultimately define both you and all you create, and every piece of work will somewhere manifest the ghost of the perpetrator. This is such a restrictive and one-dimensional place for a creative heart to be trapped.

BRINGING CLOSURE TO OPEN WOUNDS

Open wounds don't just heal. They get infected. They worsen. And if left unattended, they can even be fatal. Open wounds of any kind need closure. Ask any surgeon. Emotional closure is a very different thing to merely suppressing memories, or gallantly trying to ignore the pain. It involves cleaning out the infected area and, perhaps in extreme cases, cutting away diseased elements. This is necessary to stop the infection spreading and consuming the whole person. To live our fullest lives, and create our most meaningful and integrated art, we need to bring closure to the gashes that have cut deep into our souls. Bitterness and unforgiveness have the potential to drain the life away from us until we're incapacitated. This condition can become so overwhelming that reality begins to distort, and every attempt at creating beauty emerges in some way disfigured. For the creative heart, this is a devastating reality and one that can cause a spiral into deep depression if left unattended.

Consider how many of our creative greats have ended their own lives—evidence enough that a tortured soul isn't something to be romanticised as an inevitable part of the artist's make-up. This fallacy has caused some of our finest talents to be put on display while in states of great emotional unhealth. Hoards of vampiric consumers gorge on the raw, emotional haemorrhaging, until the collective thirst of a sea of dry, dusty souls is vicariously quenched. We seem happy to sacrifice one for the many, and it's gruesome.

NO EXCUSES

In no way am I suggesting that by forgiving the person or people who caused your Creative Wound you, therefore, must excuse what they did as being somehow okay. In many ways, I'm suggesting just the opposite. What happened mattered. It mattered a great deal. But, whether what happened resulted from a purposeful act of abuse or accidental negligence, by extending forgiveness you are actively taking back the personal power robbed from you at the time. It is an act of strength, not weakness. By rejecting passivity and denial, you transition yourself from the posture of a victim into that of a powerful, assertive artist, and one who is regaining ownership and control of their art—one decision at a time.

You see, forgiveness is rarely a one-off event. It is a choice made over and again until one day the pain is no longer there. From this moment onward, the whole subject of your wound can be engaged with from a place of newfound ease and objectivity, and the nagging pain is noticeably absent. Your creative decisions no longer have to orientate around the guiding star of hurt. And it feels good.

THE PET FOOD AISLE

When I'm shopping at the supermarket, I never go down the dog and cat food aisle. To be honest, I rarely even notice it. I don't have to force myself to ignore it, but because I don't own any pets, that aisle is not a part of my life and therefore has no place in my thoughts or feelings. In the same way, when forgiveness has its perfect work, you become so whole that the incident that once consumed your thinking, and coloured your emotions, no longer enters your head. You'll stop having to distract yourself or silently seethe behind fake smiles. Instead, like old fruit still hanging from last year's crop, the pain just naturally falls away.

RENEGOTIATE YOUR INNER VOWS

I've known people whose art is fuelled almost exclusively by the will to prove somebody else wrong. They've made inner vows that, no matter how long it takes, they will show the perpetrator just how wrong they were. But, what happens if the perpetrator never gets to see this big, creative breakthrough?

Or, what if they do notice, but treat it with flippant indifference?

That's years of effort invested in futility. Anyone who adopts this approach is on a hiding to nothing and builds a platform for another Creative Wound, likely even more devastating than the last. This new wound, compounded with all that has gone before, holds the capacity to be terminally crushing for any hope of having a satisfying creative life. Check for inner vows you may have made and be honest about what is *really* motivating your work.

FORGIVE YOURSELF

You won't need me to tell you that us creatives are notoriously adept at berating ourselves. It is so easy for us to feel intense shame or contempt for leaving ourselves vulnerable to the harm we experienced.

Even if you were culpable, to keep punishing yourself over and again by constantly reliving the moment will do little for your mental wellbeing, and is likely to damage your art in the long term. You'll become stuck and repetitive. So, find a mirror and look squarely into your own eyes; honestly admit your mistakes, then make the quality decision to forgive yourself for whatever part you played in the harm you suffered.

HOW TO KNOW YOU HAVE TRULY FORGIVEN

So, how do we know when we've truly extended forgiveness toward someone?

A good barometer for gauging this is when you can wish genuine good toward the person or people who hurt you. I realise the harm done to some of us can appear unforgivable and beyond our capacity to release, but to keep a vice-like grip onto bitterness of soul is a self-administered poison that only we ourselves can put a stop to. Forgiving doesn't cause our memories of harm to be erased, but their right to control us is actively denied. They can no longer dictate what, or under whose terms, we create.

There's no denying it can be hard to forgive when unjust things have happened. Although it has to be said that we are all capable of thinking dualistically: evaluating others by our limited understanding of their actions, and ourselves by our good intentions. So before we pass sentence as judge and jury over someone else, it is helpful to bear in mind our own areas of failure and darkness. Because, in truth, we've all needed to be forgiven by other people, many times. So, whenever I find it hard to let go, I try to draw from the well of forgiveness and grace that's been extended to me and share a cup of that.

THE BENEFITS ARE WORTH IT

The freedom that comes from forgiving brings with it a release into a whole new level of creativity. When no longer crippled by the words or actions of the mean-spirited, negligent or indifferent, you will be free to produce your truest creative work.

Forgiveness, like most worthwhile endeavours, takes significant fortitude, and you're not alone if you find the process difficult. If this describes you, then consider getting expert help from a good counsellor, spiritual director, or psychologist. They will help you understand the complexity and nuances of your wound, and help you find the best path out of the woods.

As a man who has stumbled down the road of forgiveness many times, I wholeheartedly encourage you to take the journey whenever it becomes necessary.

It's worth the trip.

Thankful Thursday

My wife, Sarah, and I have started this new thing. We call it *Thankful Thursday*. The idea is to have a complete day once a week where we ban all negative talk and only allow ourselves to speak about things we're grateful for.

Even when tough things happen on *Thankful Thursday*, we hold each other accountable to look for the good stuff.

It's not easy.

You should try it.

For example, if a driver cuts you up on the motorway, you are restricted to saying things such as, "I'm really grateful that we didn't have a collision there," as opposed to screaming blue murder at 'the idiot'.

This is a great exercise for exposing just how negative we've let ourselves become. Years of accrued disappointments can erode our positivity and dump us deep in the bog of perpetual moaning.

But, why does this even matter?

WORDS DIRECT THE WAR

The inner war we wage to bring about our creative dreams is directed and decided by our words.

The heart holds a dream: to create something beautiful. To add a brand new richness to the world. To make a one-off. To bring people joy.

The head applies its logic: our minds seem to have an infinite capacity for explaining why our ideas are silly and why we'd be a fool to even try.

The mouth is the adjudicator: in a central position between your heart and your mind is your mouth. The words you consistently choose determine the direction you'll go.

There is a brilliant piece of ancient wisdom in a passage of The Bible that compares our tongue to the rudder of a ship[1]. In comparison to the rest of the vessel, a rudder is a tiny part but its angle determines whether the ship, its cargo, and all the people on board will arrive at their desired destination or not.

The words we speak affect our emotions.

Our emotions affect our confidence.

Our confidence affects our actions.

Our actions determine whether we even start our creative project, never mind complete it.

So, while I acknowledge you've had some very painful and unjust things said to you, it's not what your mother, or your ex-husband, said that is limiting you now. It's how you've internalised and rehearsed those words, again and again, that is making the biggest impact on how your creative life is playing out today.

Because you ultimately believe yourself more than you believe anyone else.

"I could never learn to paint."

"I could never raise enough money to record an album."

"I could never start my own business."

You know what? You are right. I agree with you—because you believe your own words.

This is the soul's equivalent of the comfort eating trap: you're feeling down so you eat a fast food burger and fries. Now you feel even more down because you ate junk. So, you eat again. More junk. Ad infinitum.

You must break the cycle, or you risk getting heavier and heavier. Eventually, both body and spirit are so weighed down that they lose their ability to move.

To start breaking the cycle, try saying things like:

"I bet I could learn to paint."

"I'm sure I could find creative ways to raise enough money to record an album."

"Millions of people have started their own business. I'm going to do the same."

What if you were right? You could actually be right about what you've just dared to say. What would that mean to you? Allow yourself to consider that for a moment.

Never forget that your tongue is your rudder and that your words are steering both you and your creative life.

What do you say to that?

168 Hours

Cast your mind back to when you were just seven years old. The date is December 22nd and you're waiting for Christmas Day to arrive. Can you remember just how excruciatingly slow the passing of time took? The days felt more like weeks as the countdown ticked idly towards its festive target.

Now, transport that same seven-year-old you forward a few months, and recall the balmy summer holidays with no school. Didn't those six weeks of joyous freedom seem to pass in a flash—even quicker than the considerably shorter 72-hour run-up to Christmas Day?

What was going on there? Was time speeding up? We know that can't be true, as only God (and possibly Doctor Who) has control over time. The rest of us have little choice but to exist within the limits of its construct, unable to make it speed up or slow down, stop or start; even if we wanted it to.

Which most of us do.

Expanding or adding time to our days would be such a bonus as we all have unique demands on our time that are unavoidable. You may have children, you may have a full-time job, or you may have a member of your family who is sick and for whom you are the primary carer.

We commit to these necessary endeavours, and while not resenting them, they leave us with little margin for our creative selves. So, reluctantly, we accept that making art is something we'll never fully experience in our lives; that's the preserve of the lucky ones blessed with more time.

Time, however, is the one thing that creates a level playing field for all of us. Nobody gets more time per week than anybody else. You get 168 hours. I get 168 hours. The British Prime Minister gets 168 hours, and the newborn baby letting out her very first cry is starting her very first 168 hours, before her second week starts.

This time next week, 168 hours of your life will have passed by. Gone forever.

Of course, our individual responsibilities and commitments do vary, but not one of us is allotted even a minute of extra time to get it all done.

However, what we do get to choose is precisely where we put our focus.

FOCUS ON YOUR FOCUS

As the strain of many of our manual and repetitive jobs has eased—first by the machinery of the industrial age, and more recently by the computers of the information revolution—you'd be forgiven for thinking we were on the cusp of a wonderful utopian era.

However, in the mother of all bait-and-switch moves, it seems that technology's promise of taking the pressure off, so that our lives can finally slow down, is proving somewhat empty. As life gathers pace year-on-year, and our stress levels go through the roof, you can hear people everywhere complaining that they are busier than ever before.

One of the biggest indictments of modern society is that, instead of technology freeing us up, it is conditioning us to respond without delay to its every beck-and-call.

I'M REVOLTING

There is good news though. Despite much propaganda to the contrary, there is time available. There really is. Our problem is that we're filling it with noise. Digital distractions are new phenomena that artists of previous generations didn't have to deal with. So, let yourself off the hook for not being prepared. None of us were.

Watch as people everywhere are blissfully oblivious to all that is going on around them, their eyes glued to the warm glow of the smartphone lovingly cradled in their palm.

Suddenly, someone's phone beeps into life as a social media message insists on immediate attention. Yes! It's a new 'like' for their latest duck-pout selfie. A mini-rush of dopamine acknowledges this success by giving their addicted brain a mini celebratory high. But soon their mind settles back into neutral, anticipatory of the next hit.

This self-inflicted reality demonstrates a sobering new level of self-absorption we're encouraged to accept as normal. And people accuse artists of being self-indulgent!

Of course, you are probably not as addicted to distraction as the people I've just described, but do yourself a favour and take careful note of everything that pulls for your attention, especially if it retains your focus. Some of it may be holding you back more than you know.

Our minds are a gift to us. They are active endowments, not just passive receptors for the dumping of social media ad campaigns.

Are you, like me, ready for a creative revolution to explode into our world? One in which we take back our minds, regain our focus, reclaim ownership of our thoughts, and intentionally direct our attention?

Because, with the right focus, we can achieve a great deal in a short span of time.

You would likely not argue that Van Gogh or Mozart failed to create meaningful art with their life, would you? But did you also know they died at ages 37 and 35, respectively? Their work is revered as some of the greatest ever produced in their genre despite their available time being less than ideal.

This is our wake-up call. This—now—is our time. Our lives are happening right now.

The big question is not how do we find more time, but what consistently has our attention?

Your next 168 hours start now.

Cognitive Junk Food

Creating good art often takes time and considerable effort. It is no surprise to discover that the people who make it look easy are able to do so, not because they were born with superhuman talent, but because they've put in hours of disciplined study and practice.

It isn't just a question of having well-rehearsed motor skills, as perhaps a factory worker would demonstrate, but truly great creativity is birthed from an active, healthy, and fertile mind.

Consider for a moment our physical bodies. We know that diet and exercise form the basis of how healthy and strong we are. If we eat nothing but junk food and never move, our quality of life will doubtless suffer. So, even though you might have been born with the innate natural ability to forge a career as a professional athlete, a poor choice of food and lack of physical activity will guarantee you will never fulfil that potential.

A similar story is true regarding our creative minds. Our mental exercise and diet dictate how much of our natural potential will be fulfilled, and ultimately how much of it we will waste.

EXERCISE

This is my first book, and for some people who know me primarily as a musician, or photographer, or designer, it has been a surprise to discover I also write fairly well.

The hidden truth is that I've written a lot during my life. I've written scores of blog posts and edited award-winning educational products. I've written and edited words that have appeared in national broadsheet newspapers and crafted marketing words that convince people to buy products and services. And while I've never dreamed of being one of the writing greats, I've often had to write clear, inspiring words that accurately convey a message.

Over the years, I've been willing to get my hands dirty and work alongside writers far more skilled than myself. Some were kind, some not so much, but I made sure I learned something from each of them.

What I'm saying is this: the proposition of writing a book didn't scare me witless like it does some people, because I've been exercising myself in this area for years, and over time have built up a degree of skill, strength, and flexibility.

DIET

In order to express ourselves competently within our chosen fields, we've established that mental exercise is vital.

Now, to continue our analogy of the physical body, another necessary aspect is that of diet.

Exercise makes a body fit, but food is what nourishes the cells that make up that body. If the building blocks of the body are sickly, then the benefits of exercise won't have the longevity they might otherwise enjoy.

In terms of your creative thinking, what you feed your brain is the only raw material it has available to work with. You can predict the quality of your creative output by monitoring what you consistently put into your head.

So, if you really want to, you can choose to fill your evenings with back-to-back soap operas, and you'll have lost time you can never get back. Even worse, you now must work harder—and longer—to mine for the good stuff because you've covered all the gold with mountains of material wholly irrelevant to your art. Of course, you can appreciate the skill and effort gone into producing these shows, but does absorbing hours of them really serve you or your creative life?

What would you say to a friend who claimed to hold big creative dreams if they hampered themselves in this way?

COGNITIVE DETOX

The sticky nature of addictive entertainment is not an accident. It's purposefully designed to keep us coming back for more. The host channels can then sell high-ticket advertising to companies who are targeting us with their products.

If the penny has dropped that you've developed an un-helpful addiction to cognitive junk food, now would be a good time to do a mental detox. Rehabilitation from the need for constant entertainment will do wonders for your creative capacity. And you'll need all of that capacity if you want to fulfil your potential.

What a shame it would be to reach the final hours of your life and regret having never written the book, recorded the album, or painted the scenes you'd always dreamed would be the legacy of your life.

Will the memories of all the trash TV you've watched be much comfort to you then?

Good question.

Isn't it?

Date Nights & Deadlines

One afternoon I met a good friend for coffee. Let's call him Geoff. His name actually is Geoff, so it makes things much easier if we call him that.

Before he retired, Geoff was a project manager for a construction company. He was used to setting and reaching big goals, with large budgets (which I thought must be an unusual feeling for him, given he's a Burnley fan).

We met at one of my favourite haunts—the specialist tea & coffee house *Providero* in Llandudno. As we sat chatting, the subject of the book you're currently reading came up in conversation, and I blame the relaxed atmosphere for me not being ready for what happened next:

Geoff asked me when my book deadline was.

Oh.

Silence.

I didn't have an answer.

I'm a man who has spent years of his life leading creative people and projects, with timescales and deadlines at the very foundation of every successful project; and here was I with no finish date.

I suddenly felt acutely embarrassed. I'd been undone by a wily old professional, which was bad form considering I'd just bought him cake.

Of course, I had given a deadline for the book a few cursory thoughts but hadn't concluded anything. However, as I considered my processes, convictions and intentions, those awkward feelings lifted. Geoff had posed a necessary question for anyone starting a major creative endeavour, and I was glad he had because I learned something insightful through my answer—I'd adopted a project philosophy I hadn't consciously realised.

TIMING TRAIN WRECKS

As I'd chosen to go the indie publishing route, I didn't have a traditional publisher breathing down my neck for a finished manuscript. Also, I wasn't in a position where my livelihood depended on this book being finished. Nor was there a big speaking gig looming where I'd risk missing out on book sales. Basically, there was no time pressure being applied from anyone other than myself.

Although I've had a lot of writing experience, this is my first full book. So I had no idea what the ebbs and flows would be like, nor was I sure what a realistic time frame for completion would be. To be honest, the thought of an impending finish date made me feel like a train that would soon be careering, full-tilt, into an end-of-line station; and you can't expect to drive a locomotive into concrete-seated, solid steel buffers and come out unscathed, can you? An absolute deadline would be seriously jarring, and even tragically destructive. The project needed to be able to slow down gracefully to its conclusion.

There seemed little point setting myself up for a pointless 'failure' and the risk of an otherwise avoidable Creative Wound.

DATE NIGHT

So, rather than put myself under the pressure of a particular calendar date, I decided upon a completely different approach. It wasn't without structure, but it did relieve me of a lot of needless time pressure.

First, I scrapped the idea of circling a date in my calendar for when the project had to come screeching to a self-imposed halt. Instead, I blocked out an hour every evening, purely for thinking and writing. At 8:30 pm, when my little girl was asleep in bed, my phone would flash up a useful reminder that book creation hour was underway.

I didn't even have a rule that I had to write, or even stick to an hour, but I knew if I engaged with that time during the majority of evenings, then this book wouldn't do anything other than eventually end up finished.

So I put an end to the impending doom of an absolute target date and turned my book creation process into a regular date night with myself, which was a much more agreeable proposition.

If your creative project isn't served well by a cast-iron deadline date, simply choose to not live under the dictates of one. Sometimes they do help, especially when you're working on a project that isn't a labour of love, but as artists we rarely need that extra motivation; in fact, the pressure of it can sometimes serve only to paralyse.

Giving yourself a regular gift of focus time is much more likely to result in an enjoyable creative session, where work still gets done along with the bonus of not stressing yourself out.

Adopting this approach helps me shift my perspective from being a 'half empty' to a 'half full' one. The traditional deadline model would have forced my focus to be on how much I still needed to write before a fast-approaching arbitrary day arrived. But by having date nights instead, I enjoyed personal mini-celebrations as each evening led to more pages being written.

DEATH OF THE DEADLINE

For many years I've taken on board Dr. Steven R. Covey's famous and eminently helpful ethos of starting every new project with the end result in mind. Here, the end I had in mind was to have a completed book I was proud of, filled with inspirational thoughts that were helpful to fellow battlers in the creative trenches.

I didn't want to rush it. I didn't have to rush it. I was happy for it to be finished when it was finished.

Of course, this approach doesn't work for every kind of project. You can't expect to overshoot magazine illustration cut-off dates and then blame it on me. But, if you are deadline-free when making your art, then adding artificial constraints may cause you to rush without good reason, and the quality of your final work will suffer.

For many years I have tracked my work and personal life commitments using David Allen's *GTD (Getting Things Done)* method, a system which has achieved a cult-like following since he launched his book *Getting Things Done: The Art of Stress-Free Productivity* in 2001. I enjoy working this way as it brings clarity and perspective to all I'm committed to. But, I also issue a cautionary note if you adopt this, or any of the other popular productivity methods.

As much as I love and use them, I've found structured productivity systems encourage lapses into the 'factory mindset' of cranking out as much of whatever it is I'm making. I then label that as being optimal productivity when in reality it is anything but.

So, while I encourage the use of systems and structure within your life and work, these must always directly serve your vision and actively support your goals. Otherwise, your creative freedom will capitulate as your life descends into a box-ticking frenzy.

HEADSPACE

Sometimes, just sitting and thinking is the most productive thing you can do.

"Now, Brenda, you go sit down this afternoon and have yourself a good old think."

Not the kind of thing you're likely to hear from your typical 9–5 boss is it?

When working on creative projects that you fully own, be sure to give yourself that gift: space to think. It has untold potential to release you into new depths of expressive freedom.

So if you'd like to produce the best art you are capable of, and you want to finish it for others to experience, enjoy and benefit from, experiment with *not* setting a deadline. Have a date night with yourself instead. (Just don't tell the productivity experts what you're up to).

So I explained these thoughts to Geoff; and before he could ask me any more searching questions, I distracted him with more cake and asked how well he thought Burnley would do this season...

Don't Patronise Me, I'm Starving

Laura met an interesting woman at a party in downtown LA. During their conversation, the woman shared her story of how she moved there 10 years ago in pursuit of her dream. That dream was of being a Hollywood movie star—something she'd held as a treasure in her heart since childhood. Laura listened intently to the narrative. It covered worldwide acknowledgement of her acting ability, the great adoration of her fans, and a huge fortune amassed along the way. Eventually, the woman handed the conversation back over to Laura and it was her turn to speak:

"Oh, that's great!" she exclaimed, "Which restaurant are you a waitress for?"

This irreverent tale always creates wry smiles as heads nod knowingly because there is something that seems so true about it. In one sense it's amusing, but it's also sad, and really quite tragic. It's the story of a dreamer who didn't see her dream fulfilled. Not only that, but it had been switched for years of mundane, low-paid work, serving people who only noticed her when there was something wrong with their food.

The starving artist paradigm is, unfortunately, a commonly held notion. It often carries with it a romanticised idea that true artists create solely for the love of it, and never, ever for money. So, the line goes that for you to be remunerated in any way, you must be selling out and engaging in a crude abandonment of your true artistic calling; choosing to sully your name, and that of all other creatives, in an act of wilful degradation of the purity of your art.

Being on the receiving end of such disparaging disapproval isn't pleasant and is something you may have experienced. I know I have. Perhaps you've even uttered such words yourself, even directing them *at* yourself. But, is it actually true? For art to be legitimate, does the creator have to be poor? Does real art always come from a place of scarcity and suffering? Is it possible to spend time creating what you love and not be left destitute? Are these things mutually exclusive?

If you dare to think otherwise, well-meaning people will try to convince you you're not being realistic, and encourage you to stop living in a dream world.

Stories of Creative Wounds abound here.

THE CURSE OF POVERTY

In 1943, Abraham Maslow presented his paper *A Theory of Human Motivation*, based on the prioritisation of human need. Often presented as a hierarchical pyramid, it charts the progression from basic physiological needs such as food, water, shelter and rest, through several stages to the pinnacle of self actualisation, which is the stage when creativity thrives.

If you are fighting to survive from day to day, and are focused on the bottom tier of Maslow's hierarchy of needs, you don't naturally think to spend much time indulging in the arts. Instead, your mind is consumed with how to meet the next round of bills, and your creative energy is spent dreaming up better ways to stretch out your meagre income.

You simply don't have the headspace or time for creation—certainly not the type that brings your heart alive. Remember how you used to explore, experiment, and lose yourself in newfound depths within your chosen discipline? Instead, these days, you are stressed-out by the limits on your time, and you're becoming increasingly bored with how repetitive you've become.

You can claim it's how your style has developed if you like, but deep down you know the truth. Your time and energy have been stolen by your constant need to chase money to pay nameless, faceless corporations for the essential utilities that sustain your modern lifestyle.

The guitarist resorts to playing the same old licks he's played for the past 20 years. An artist paints familiar, tired strokes with the same safe hues. A writer dries up after her first book because her soul has had no time to breathe.

Creativity-by-numbers slowly drains your spirit until depression engulfs you, and you just quit. You can congratulate yourself for trying, of course. You gave art a go. And at least you starved—so you must've been the real deal.

In reality, you're stymied by lack.

And it hurts.

HAVE YOU GOT THE SKILLS TO PAY THE BILLS?

You have likely heard the old adage 'It takes money to make money'. Is that something you believe to be true?

I used to, and it was a killer.

I grew up in a humble household in a humble town. We had little money, and the pervading mindset was that I shouldn't ever expect this to change.

I was part of the working class, living in the back-end of nowhere, and we didn't have the money to make money. So that was that—destined to a life bobbing around the poverty line with no prospects of it improving.

Yes, lack of money was a problem, but far worse was the crippling belief that improvement was impossible.

Imagine if Richard Branson, the epitome of the self-made

millionaire, had believed this back in 1970 when he first started in business. Who knows what he'd be doing today. He purportedly began with the princely sum of £300, and his current fortune is estimated to be around £3.6 billion. That's a decent return in anyone's book! You could argue that he did use *some* money to make money—but in reality, this wasn't the governing factor in his success. Creativity, ingenuity, and looking beyond himself to help others made the difference.

Of course, if you're printing a book, pressing CDs, or opening an art gallery, there is inevitably a financial cost involved. Sometimes a large one. And if you find yourself in a place where your bank balance isn't in a strong enough position to support your project then that could put you out of the game.

I know a lot of creatives who have given up at this point.

In his book *Outliers*, Malcolm Gladwell argues that for any skill to be developed to an expert level, it typically takes an individual 10,000 hours of focused learning and applied practice. If this is true, then it can be incredibly hard for the poverty-line artist to hone their skills adequately in a quick enough timeframe. They're too busy working multiple dead-end jobs in order to survive.

Wonderful, inspiring, life-changing pieces of creative genius are imprisoned in perpetuity simply because the artist can't afford to create.

Some people work multiple jobs so they can be creative

in the few spare hours that remain. But you know that approach wouldn't allow you adequate time or space to improve as much as you need.

The message to your heart can be crippling: "It's okay for those who've made it. Those who get paid to create. You know, the professionals. But that's not me."

"Besides, it's not real art if I get paid for it, is it? After all, none of the great painters from centuries past had their artwork licensed for huge billboard ad campaigns, did they?"

Well, no. Of course, they didn't. But, is it true that they made their art without anybody paying them?

And, what if you were freed up enough from money worries so that your creativity could flow?

Let's investigate.

TURNER

It was likely because of my grandma's influence that I loved painting as a child. And I don't mean poster paints and a cheap plastic brush, I mean with oils and a palette knife—at age seven. Back in the days before video recorders, my brother and I would furiously argue over TV channels. He'd want something action packed like *Starsky & Hutch,* whereas I didn't want to miss *Paint Along With Nancy!* I wasn't a typical child.

Anyway, my love of art led me to become a little infatuated by J. M. W. Turner during my college years, and I made several pilgrimages down to the Tate Gallery in London to see his work in person. If you're not familiar, I encourage you to at least look up *The Fighting Temeraire*. It's one of Turner's most celebrated paintings, and one of my favourites.

A quick and enjoyable way to get a feel for his life is the movie *Mr Turner*, in which Timothy Spall brilliantly brings the character of Turner to life. You'll learn just how much the 1800s art world hinged on commissions and the financial support of patrons. Wealthy individuals paid artists large sums of money for their paintings. This released the artists from the worry of how they'd meet their basic needs (at least), freeing them up to produce better and more abundant, creative works. Many of these paintings are still being enjoyed today, years after their creators' passing.

BEETHOVEN

The same pattern emerges throughout the arts. Take composer Ludwig van Beethoven, for example. He made money through the publication of his compositions as well as public performances of his work. That's a concept not too far removed from playing gigs and licensing music for a TV show, is it? Plus, he also relied heavily on the generosity of a handful of patrons. A few deeply invested individuals were hugely significant in the music Beethoven created. He didn't have millions of social media followers or the financial backing of a big corporation. Instead, he created relationships with individuals who loved his work, believed in him, and were willing and able to invest.

I see the art world heading this way again—away from the grasp of multinational corporations back into the care of the people. Because of the connecting power of the internet, creators and appreciators can again meet person to person and collaborate without the permission of a board of directors whose main aim is to maximise profits.

RECLAIM THE LOST MAGIC OF THE GOLDEN YEARS

A friend of mine, James, was once signed to a major record label and spent two years recording an album which the label then decided not to release. Compounding this disappointment further is the fact the album forever belongs to the label, and James can't make any use of the recordings he invested 24 months of his life into. I heard a couple of the tracks in his home studio once, and they sounded wonderful. Tastefully musical songs, expertly played with a gorgeous sonic quality, captured in several of the UK's finest recording studios. And nobody will ever get to hear them. Unless you're me. Or James's cat.

In the golden years of the record label, artists were given multi-album deals and years with which to develop, mature, and grow in their craft. Today, the tiny number of newly signed artists are under pressure to be an instant hit or be discarded like an old pair of shoes.

However, I believe we can take back some of the magic that

has been lost. We can give ourselves the gift of time and space in which to develop, and look back on the journey of our development with a sense of real accomplishment.

Couple that with the relief felt from not having to pay back hundreds of thousands of pounds in advance money, and the revelation dawns as to what a blessed time we live in.

We can all now create and sell our own art without having to ask anybody's permission. Creativity truly is transitioning back into the hands of the people.

Grab a hold!

Perfectionism & Play

The empty sleeve of Grandad's tweed jacket brushed against the strings of my acoustic guitar. It was the lightest of touches, but still enough to deaden all vibration and unexpectedly launch me into an impromptu a capella performance.

Argh!

Exposing my formative singing voice to public scrutiny was the last thing I'd intended.

It was 1981, and this was my first public performance—singing a few songs for extended family at our annual Boxing Day gathering, which always took place at my grandparents' country farm cottage. And, despite what it sounded like, this wasn't expressive vibrato in my voice. No, sir. This was fear. The whole of my eight-year-old frame involuntarily trembled as the room fell silent in readiness of absorbing every sound I was about to make.

This whole experience presented itself as a strange new dichotomy: the desire for someone to hear my music, yet an aversion to anyone watching and listening. This matter wasn't improved any when a rush of pre-performance adrenaline placed all the senses of my juvenile frame into an uncomfortable state of red-alert.

So, when it came to choosing the stage for my seminal debut concert, I opted for… the cupboard under the stairs. Here I could hide behind a plush coat-and-hat barricade, which provided ample protection against the doting gaze of aunties and uncles, many of whom I wasn't even convinced were actual relatives.

My musical references at the time were '70s musical giants such as *Queen, Simon & Garfunkel,* and *Dire Straits*—artists I'd regularly hear being played on the stereo at home. But the combination of intense nerves, my pre-pubescent larynx, and ill-advised song choices, conspired to serve up such crowd-pleasing gems as *We're All Going To The Zoo Tomorrow* in the style of a vaseline-gargling chipmunk. Or, at least that's how it felt.

Everybody loved it of course, in the way you love a puppy doing its first tricks. But I didn't want to be 'good for my age', I wanted to be good. So, the fight was on.

And over thirty years later, it still is.

THE DRIVE TO BE PERFECT

Whenever we're exposed or knocked down, our instinctive

response is to do all we can to avoid a further repeat. This makes sense because nobody in their right mind wants to resubmit themselves to harm, do they? But, as a result, we can hold our work back for far too long, not daring to invite critique or comment until all potential threats have been preemptively deflected.

Round in circles we go, striving to control every variable: tweaking, changing, revising, and nudging. We spin ever faster on the spot in an obsessive, twirling frenzy—until we've whisked the distinctive colours of our work into a mushy splodge.

Although understandable on one level, perfectionism is exhausting. We exchange the thrill of wild, untamed imagination for a binary system of right or wrong; perfect or flawed. Yes, following these rules and conventions appears safe—requiring little risk, clever thinking or inventive application—but it's ultimately soulless; all we need do is develop the right techniques and follow the instructions; and if our creation fails, then we can blame it on the system, even if the system and its rules exist nowhere but inside our head.

Aiming for perfect, we end up with safe: great when buying a family car but rarely the dream for our art.

Perfectionism is a blade through the heart of wonder.

As creators, whatever we produce automatically contains the essence of who were are, and is often accompanied by the dread that our work is about to expose our inadequacies to the world. Are you fearful of making less-than-perfect art because it would mark you as being a deficient person? If that line of thinking is true, what does creating nothing at all make you?

HAVE FUN FAILING

Being aware that change is possible makes it easier to endure difficult times with our art. This requires imagination. But the brain's ability to imagine is inhibited when experiencing higher-than-normal stress levels. So, if we habitually dwell on our moments of trauma, we limit our ability to see alternate possibilities beyond our current circumstance because we are reliving our pain, heightening our stress, and inhibiting our capacity for imagination.

To break out of this cycle, we must reawaken the areas of the brain that process possibility and imagination, and for help with that we should take a leaf from the book of the world experts: children.

It seems counterintuitive, and likely one of the last things you want to do when striving to make your best work, but the antidote to the shackles of perfectionism is to stop all work for a while and just play.

As a 'grown up' it might feel like a regression to lose yourself in mischief and fun, but to do so is vital for getting free.

True play allows us to disengage and step back from the intense, obsessive focus on our work. Here we reacquaint ourselves with the delights of improvisation and exploration, without the pressure to perform or reach anybody's standards, including our own.

In short, when done properly, play is unbridled freedom, a place where stress dissipates and our ability to imagine reignites.

Play is too serious for us to ignore.

EMBRACE A CURIOUS ADVENTURE

In a bold move during the summer of 2015, Sarah and I put all work on hold for six weeks and flew 23 hours and 10,560 miles from Heathrow Airport, London to Sydney, Australia.

You might wonder why our bumper holiday belongs in a book about creativity, and you'd be right to ask, it's a good question. Well, here's the thing: for Sarah and I, creativity is more than just 'doing art and music for a job'. Instead, it is fundamental to our posture of heart toward life as a whole. Living this way—one creative choice at a time—is a major factor in us both having reservoirs of liquid inspiration on-tap, which we both frequently need in our work.

While discussing taking a trip down under, we could easily have reasoned that this was a luxury we couldn't afford. To take a large chunk of time away from the studio would mean I'd have no income during that period. Likewise, as Sarah wouldn't be teaching her regular piano students, neither would she.

Although we had some savings nestled away in a bank account, these mainly came as a small inheritance from the will of Sarah's much-loved grandfather, so it mattered immensely how that money was used.

How, exactly, does a creative person celebrate the memory of a beloved relative with appropriate gratitude?

It's in moments like this that you're met, again, with choice: either keep your creativity chained to the treadmill and force it to keep on producing, or treat it to the rejuvenating trip of a lifetime. Just as a wise farmer periodically allows his fields to lie fallow, you'll love the fruitfulness that follows a season of deep rest.

So, for us, the answer was only ever going to be an investment into the heart. An investment into joy. To create a life experience and carve out memories. To establish new and deeper connections between us as a couple through a dramatic shared experience while dedicating every moment of it as an unforgettable memorial.

Or we could just stay at home.

OPEN YOUR EYES

I'll never forget witnessing the birth of a new day as we sliced through the sun-torched clouds on our descent into Sydney airport. In response, the Pacific Ocean reflected back this celestial glory, and our plane was engulfed on all sides by a shimmering dance of water and light. It was one of the most magnificent things I'd ever seen.

That, my friend, was enough to inspire the poet in anybody.

And forget trying to video it on your phone. If you ever find yourself filming a magnificent moment and are only experiencing its fleeting grandiosity through a tiny screen, in all honesty, you missed it. You didn't live it. There's no other rational choice at this point but to open up every sense as wide as you can and just soak it in.

Not everybody saw it, either. They were packing bags, reading, talking. Open eyes but blank stares missed the whole dazzling exhibition.

It is possible to have your eyes open but not see a thing.

BE PRESENT

If you are fully present, little else has the potency of an entirely new experience for unlocking your creative curiosity. When faced with unusual circumstances you can either recoil into a familiar, safe environment or push into new things. It always takes somebody somewhere to push into new things so that others can follow. Why shouldn't that be you?

It wasn't so long ago that a fast horse was the pinnacle of transport speed and luxury, but here we were, sitting over eight miles above the surface of the earth and hurtling along at nearly 600 miles per hour. Doesn't the notion of that, alone, provoke a sense of wonder?

So I urge you to open your eyes. Look—really look—at the world. You can't fail to be inspired.

OBSERVE & ABSORB

Not long into our extended stay in Australia I decided to document the experience and the new things I'd learned; and, beyond recording facts, I wanted to capture the feeling of being there.

Photographs and smartphone videos are a useful aide memoir, but the 'great holiday snaps show' is often boring for the people who weren't there. Their emotional centre just doesn't connect with the meaning that the images have personally to you.

But, as our trip was laden with new experiences, I wanted to capture the emotions these experiences created. So, instead of relying on a few photos, I wrote a few short pieces so we could share our adventure with friends back home.

I came to relish the daily rhythm of popping out of the campervan every morning to go and write in a local coffee shop. Meanwhile, Sarah enjoyed some much-needed space away from me!

And so I continued to write.

(I have included a few of these short tales at the back of the book in *Australian Memoirs.*)

THE RIGHT TO WRITE

As a boy, I loved books, and words in general. I remember being aged 10 when my English teacher gave me a copy of George Orwell's *1984* to read as an extra-curricular treat, and from a young age I considered writing as a possible career path. I once even won a small, local literary award. And although a writing for a living wasn't how it panned out, much of my early career required a good grasp of English. However, over time, the reams of uninteresting subject matter that passed in front of my eyes steadily eroded my desire to write. I even forgot how much I'd once loved it.

So, it was to my immense surprise that 30 years later, on an impromptu coffee shop tour of Australia, crafting sentences was bringing me actual joy again. The trip had helped me to re-frame what writing meant, from being a necessity of my working life, back to being pure fun. I'd often sit unashamedly giggling into my coffee as I typed up funny memories from our trip. And as I connected with the emotions of the experience, dormant parts of my creative self were reawakening. It helped greatly that I wasn't depending on these words to provide any form of income, and I needed nobody's approval.

It was exhilarating.

This renewed excitement for writing, reborn by taking my curiosity on a wild adventure, was the catalyst for this book. So, I heartily encourage you, too, to do something you've never done before, and take note of how your soul responds. Then, at the intersection where your life meets the new experience, use these feelings as fuel and inspiration to create something brand new.

I suggest you carry a notebook or instal a note-taking

app on your phone, and record those moments when the world, your thoughts, and circumstances converge and arouse new intrigue. When established ideas collide, they create new things. A new thought. A new idea—at the very least, a new idea to you. But if you don't catch it quickly, you will watch in fascination as it dances like a butterfly on the breeze before disappearing forever.

The thing is, we don't encounter these moments by doing faultless work. We catch them by being present, open, interested and aware.

So, punch perfectionism in the face and choose to see your work—and your life—as the big, wonder-inducing adventure playground that it really is.

Meet You In Melbourne

Sarah and I had been trying for a baby for two years. Our desire to create a brand-new life was met month upon month with compounding disappointment, and we didn't know why. We'd suffered all manner of undignified medical tests and intrusions and, although nothing was found to be wrong, something clearly wasn't right.

We asked about going through an IVF (In Vitro Fertilisation) program but learned that a new policy had just been introduced in Wales, and we'd missed the cut-off date by less than a month. It would be another full year's wait until they would even consider us for an initial conversation. This latest bombshell dropped on us from within our consultant's office—a cupboard, barely adequate for a single person into which three of us had manoeuvred, along with two (thankfully quite svelte) junior doctors. My unavoidable knee-to-knee brushes with the young man opposite did nothing to lighten the awkward tension of discussing my sperm, and how nobody could do anything to help us for at least twelve more months.

This is a unique kind of Creative Wound. It gnaws at the core of your personhood like nothing else and brings the whole validity of your existence into question if you let it. *What's wrong with me? What's wrong with us? How come our friends are having children and we can't manage it? Are we doing something wrong?* Questions cascaded down into an ever-deepening pool of "Why?"

During this period, one of Sarah's friends gave her a book—a risky move given the sensitivity of our situation, but one we're glad she had the nerve to take. This book was called *God's Plan For Pregnancy,* by Nerida Walker. Now, before you panic and adopt the brace position, a Bible-bashing will not happen from me. However, there is a story to tell. It's what author Elizabeth Gilbert might refer to as *Big Magic* in her book of the same name. As we pursued our curiosity, and took some risks to follow the voice of our hearts, something quite remarkable unfolded. This is the kind of thing that happens to other people, not us; except that it did.

We'd both devoured Nerida's inspiring book, and took heart from the many accounts of fruitfulness despite medical prognoses of certain barrenness, including Nerida and husband Shaun's own family story. This lifted our hopes to believe us having a baby was still possible even though nothing seemed to be changing. So, instead of putting our lives into permanent stasis, we decided to keep living as fully as possible, a factor that helped validate our dream of road-tripping around Australia.

As anybody who knows her will testify, Sarah loves anything Aussie, and when we discovered Nerida lived there it instantly won her a couple of extra points! So, with Nerida's Facebook page[1] duly followed, we got on with everyday life and the task of booking flights and a campervan, ready to explore Australia.

TO MELBOURNE AND BACK

We picked up our *Hippie Hitop* campervan from just outside Sydney, and planned our 14-day road trip thus, "Let's drive to Melbourne and back." I don't remember us planning much more than that. We'd wake up, drive, and explore when the notion grabbed us. Then we'd pull in for the night at the most convenient campsite.

As we journeyed south, part of our daily hunt involved finding decent WiFi hotspots. Not every campsite had one, and the ones that did weren't always a byword for reliability. Before long, we discovered that the Golden Arches of *McDonald's* offered the most consistent internet connection, and as they appeared with ubiquity along our trail, they soon became the regular watering hole for quenching our digital connectivity thirst.

It was during one such half-hour internet stop-off that the magic started, two days' drive away from our Melbourne destination.

The first part of the tale begins with an old school friend, Colette. She and her family had emigrated to Melbourne a few years earlier, and on hearing that Sarah and I would be in the area, steamrolled us with kind offers of hospitality. I'd planned on us perhaps meeting for a quick coffee, but she was having none of that. Colette insisted we abandoned all intention of staying at a campsite once we reached Melbourne, offering us a room in their family home instead. We gratefully accepted. A comfortable bed was too good to refuse, and I was excited to meet with a friend I'd not seen since we were both spotty, gangly teenagers with little clue about anything. And, after 25 years, it was good to see at least our acne had cleared up.

The second part of this curious tale transpired as Sarah's Facebook feed delivered news that an impromptu public meeting would be taking place with the aforementioned author, Nerida Walker, in Melbourne. Amazingly, the venue was less than twenty minutes from my friend Colette's house. Now, this is where it gets almost incredulous. I hardly believe it myself, and I was there. Nerida hadn't visited Melbourne for over six years and would be flying in for *one night only—the very evening Sarah and I were to arrive!*

Now, if we could have chosen one person in the world to share the pain of our situation with at that time, it would have been Nerida Walker. And in the freakiest of divine timetabling, our lives were about to converge at a single moment in time, through no plan or intention of our own. And, remember, this pinpoint accuracy was taking place in a country so vast that you can fly 600 miles-per-hour for five hours and still not leave its boundaries.

Under no circumstances were we going to miss this meeting.

Arriving over two hours early, we parked the campervan in the church car park and got some rest to boost our batteries for whatever was about to follow. There are some occasions when you honestly don't know what to expect. This was one of those.

The event was low key, and no more than 30 other people joined us in a chilly, ancillary meeting room in which a couple of rickety fan heaters fought to raise the temperature a degree or two.

As Nerida quizzed the room as to where everyone had come from, we had fun interrupting the list of local Melbourne suburbs with shouts of "North Wales!" It took a couple of times before they actually believed us. Our funny accents probably helped.

Nerida did as much to warm everybody up as the heaters did, candidly sharing parts of her own family story. This inspired a lot of hope in those of us present. We heard how she and Shaun have now got four children, to the disbelief of the medical world, as Shaun's medical diagnosis was that of being clinically sterile. What I adore about this story is that nobody ever raises the question of fatherhood as all the children so strongly resemble their dad.

After the talk, Sarah and I enjoyed good conversation, and a fine buffet, with other people there that night; and Nerida took the time to pray for us—believing we would experience the fruitfulness we so desired.

I'm not sure you can witness such an intricate set of circumstances coming together with such meticulous precision and not feel an extra gust of wind in your sails. The whole thing gave us renewed belief and an even greater resolve to not stop trying.

BACK HOME

A few weeks later, we returned to the UK, and normal everyday life resumed. Months came and went, along with the familiar old cycle of heartbreak.

So, what was that all about in Australia? Did it even mean anything? At times it all felt like a big, cruel joke. Until, one morning, Sarah came into our bedroom and just stared at me—unable to speak. I was worried that something terrible had happened as she was in a state of shock I'd never seen her in before.

She held up a pregnancy test strip. Positive.

The next morning she did another test. Positive.

The next morning we used a different brand. Positive.

On it went until I finally put my foot down. You know you're going too far when the choice to buy more pregnancy tests hampers your ability to afford food. So, we just had to believe it was true. Sarah was actually pregnant; and nine months later we welcomed our new baby girl into the world.

After much protracted heartache, we experienced our dream fulfilled. It had meant us going on a mammoth, disruptive, and adventurous trip around the world; miraculously meeting someone who had trodden this path before us, and who was also willing to stand shoulder-to-shoulder with us in believing for a change—a change we'd been powerless to bring about on our own.

Now, I'm not saying you have to accept something divine occurred here, although I certainly do. I'm just telling you what happened. This happened. It involved no planning and no strategy on our part. There were too many moving pieces for us to orchestrate anything so complex. We simply adopted a willingness to have fun and go exploring with big, open, hope-filled hearts, choosing to believe the maker of the universe has designed it to work in our favour.

YOU ARE ONE DAY CLOSER

So, whatever it is you desire to give birth to, especially if it seems painfully elusive, let me encourage you to keep going in your pursuit.

Be unswerving. Be relentless.

This is your art. Your life. There's never been another you, so don't squander your big chance to make your mark.

Stay curious and go on adventures. Use the pain of your

Creative Wound to work in your favour. Keep your eyes and ears open for vital clues, and never, ever stop believing.

Today, you are one day closer.

Finish Something

Starting isn't the hardest part.

Anecdotal and scientific evidence converge in overwhelming agreement—it is harder to see something through than to start something new.

Every New Year's Day, millions of us make a new start. Yet research from The University Of Stanton suggests that only 8% of people stay committed to their New Year resolutions.[1] That leaves a staggeringly high percentage of people who start but don't finish.

Even if your current creative project isn't your most satisfying, do all you can to finish it. Simply seeing a project through to the end sets you apart from the masses.

Commit to finishing whatever you start. Or, put another way, always keep your word. Keep your word to others. Keep your word to yourself. Over time, you will abandon far fewer projects and complete far more. You will return calls when you say you will and show up when you've promised. Do this and your self-esteem will soar.

This is more a question of integrity than motivation. Goal setting and good intentions are woefully inadequate if we don't strengthen our resolve to value and keep our own word.

I have an aspiration to be the most reliable person I know. Of course, in reality, I am far from perfect, but even if keeping my word proves inconvenient, I will do my best to keep it. I consider how I'd like to be treated if I were on the receiving end, and ask myself what kind of man I want to be. That is usually enough to confirm which course of action I should be taking.

An unswerving commitment to finishing what you start also helps when choosing what to start in the first place. When your "yes" really does mean "yes" then starting a project instigates a bond of commitment toward it. Your time, energy, and resources are automatically accounted for and are subsequently off limits to anyone or anything else.

Of course, on occasion, things do have to be renegotiated, but when a commitment to keeping your word becomes your default mode, renegotiations are rare exceptions rather than the rule.

I've lost count how many times well-intentioned people have made promises to help me with something, or agreed to be somewhere at a certain date and time, and have forgotten. Even though they are entirely sincere in the moment, they lack resolve, and don't hold their own words in high enough esteem to watch over them with any degree of diligence. It gets to where, even though I enjoy their company and value them as people, I simply can't afford to believe them or trust their promise.

This is something we must pay attention to, as, if we're not careful, we can inflict ourselves with the same disrespectful behaviour. We promise ourselves we'll commit to a new creative project and are excited to see the finished work, but there's no genuine conviction behind our words. We are just people pleasing—and in the most tragic of hoodwinking manoeuvres, we speak to placate ourselves.

It's an enlightening and sobering day when we're honest enough to admit that we can't trust our own word to ourselves. However, this is something we can change—and must change—if our desire for a restored creative heart is to have any chance of success.

START AGAIN BEFORE YOU FINISH

Bringing any piece of art or creative project to completion can be a highly emotional experience, sometimes even evoking a kind of grief. Like when parents are left alone as children leave the family home, there is genuine joy and also deep sadness.

A similar dynamic can happen at retirement. It is possible to spend years working toward the goal of having more free time, only to be presented at the zenith with an infinite expanse of "Now what?"

Recall reaching the end of a film, or book, that you were deeply engrossed in. The ending jolts you out of your dream state, dumping you in an ethereal haze of empti-ness. I remember when the final sentence of *The Lord Of The Rings* trilogy slipped under the gaze of my eyes, and I closed the cover for the last time. I felt a deep sorrow that it was all over. An entire world had just ended, as if a black hole had swallowed everything up in an instant, leaving nothingness in its stead.

Completing any creative endeavour can leave you feeling the same way because the work is connected to a deep part of your soul. Your mind has been consumed with one thing, and this one thing has enchanted you for a long time, but now it's all over. So, you sit there in silence, wondering if there is anything more. Questioning, "Will I ever love again?"

As you bring your works to completion, know you will almost certainly experience this kind of reaction. It doesn't mean there is anything wrong, it's just that something great has reached its conclusion, and you're now in transition. It's hard to let go, especially if it has been an enjoyable experience, but this period is now over. So, celebrate the life of the work and the time you spent together. It's okay to mourn a little, but recognise that the time to move on is here.

One technique I've discovered to get over this kind of

slump is to start something new before a current major work is complete. This way, I'm not left floundering offshore in a sea of aloneness, but instead I'm able to transfer my focus seamlessly onto the next exciting thing. I think of it like a relay race—there is always a point where two runners are engaged at full pace in order for the baton to be passed on. You might find this approach worth experimenting with.

Alternatively, if you're burned out, give yourself some downtime—like a farmer allows a field to lie fallow for a season. Maybe have a mini-break, visit friends, spend time in nature—do whatever brings restoration to your soul.

The overall point I'm making is for you to be aware that an endpoint is always coming, and it is wise to prepare your next move so you don't sink into an otherwise avoidable funk.

IF I DON'T FINISH YOU CAN'T JUDGE ME

Sometimes we don't finish what we're working on because we dread the criticism and judgement that might follow when we finally let go. So, if we never get done, we will never be vulnerable to the thoughts and opinions of others. By thinking this way, it is easy to become a perennial tweaker, convincing ourselves that we won't get hurt if we don't complete. But this ends up hurting us more, because it keeps us rooted in a stuck place—unable to move on or begin anything new. By not finishing, we ensure that we will never learn, develop, or grow to anything like the degree we are capable of.

This is why we must commit to finishing things.

Ultimately, the creative life is about our growth, maturity and learning, far more than reaching a linear goal of being 'the best'—whatever that might mean. And to finish is often an act of great courage, especially if you've suffered unkindness in response to previous creative offerings.

And the good news is you're never really done—not if you don't want to be. Even if the last time was an irrefutable disaster, you get to go again. Because, rather than a continuous, straight journey, the creative life is more like a series of revolutions. It is cyclical, and rhythmic, and yet intensely progressive.

Like a record player.

A 33-inch vinyl spins on the turntable as you lower the needle gently into the groove, causing the speakers to release a subtle hum, hiss, and crackle into the air. Without this contact, the record revolves in silence, with little purpose to its continual circular motion.

But by dropping the needle, making a connection and commitment, it conspires with the spinning record to produce sound. So, even though the record still goes round in circles, the needle makes resolute progress on its journey across the spiralled surface, as together they release music.

Going round in circles doesn't necessarily mean you're going round in circles.

THE BEGINNING AND THE END

I've lived most of my adult life in the historic UK city of York. The centrepiece of the city's architecture is York Minster, a majestic Gothic Cathedral, which took 250 years to complete. Work began in 1220 and the building was finally completed in 1472.[2]

The commitment to build York Minster is an impressive feat given that many of the architects, stonemasons, glaziers, and others involved knew they'd never see the final results of their labour.

Mature imaginations serve a bigger picture than the immediate by valuing the longevity and legacy of their creative work. In the case of York Minster, that work would ultimately become a beacon to draw communities together in a place of transcendent beauty, and which—over 500 years later—still reverently echoes the awesomeness of God.

In our culture of the instant and disposable, I wonder how it would feel to begin a creative project, destined to be one of the most celebrated and monumental of its kind in the whole of Europe, knowing you would never lay eyes on its completion?

Everything begins and everything ends. And it is healthy to acknowledge that these necessary constraints actually help define our art. Every painting is limited by its canvas. Every piece of music has an opening and a close—whether it be the two-minute pop songs of the Beatles, or John

Cage's Organ Project in Halberstadt, Germany—which is set to last for an unprecedented 639 years.[3]

There is a tremendous comfort knowing the creative cycle perpetually offers new beginnings, although these can only manifest in the spaces vacated by other works as they are completed. So, begin every new project knowing that—no matter how great it is—at some point this, too, will end. It's just a lot more satisfying to finish something with intention than being forced to abandon it.

So, dare to drop your needle in the groove and connect with the spinning. Commit to the journey of reaching the end of whatever you make your connection with.

Go finish something.

Conclusion

It is my hope that, through reading this book, you have formed a clear picture of the regions of the soul we must labour within to recover from an assault on our creative lives. And, my friend, there truly is hope: recovery and restoration are intrinsic to the nature of the world we live in. Whenever I cut my finger, it doesn't stay open and bleeding. If I clean the wound, put a plaster on it, and exercise a little patience, very soon I'll not even remember I'd had a wound at all. Even the devastation caused by a vast forest fire can be hard to detect a few years after the event. In fact, there is compelling evidence to suggest that a fire can actually be beneficial to the long-term health of a forest, ridding it of harmful competition for resources.[1]

Of course, one read-through of a little book like this won't instantly revolutionise everything. But we've mapped out some rough terrain together and traversed some arduous regions, and through it have gained vital orientation, gathered new insights and tools, and reminded ourselves of wisdom we'd long forgotten, all of which will aid us on our pilgrimage. And this is the crux—pilgrimage. It is nothing less than a holy journey to go from broken to whole. For many years, I have loved a particular passage in Psalm 84 of the Bible. It exhorts us to journey through the valley of tears because, in doing so, we will go from strength to strength *if we fix our hearts on pilgrimage.*[2]

This pilgrimage toward healing our broken art is like going on a round-the-world tour and picking up items distinctive to each place, becoming more experienced and well-rounded as we go. For fine wine and gourmet food, visit France. For castles and historic houses, visit the UK. For kangaroos in the wild, visit Australia. And so it is with the journey of the creative heart—to get what we need, *we must go there.* I'm unaware of any shortcuts or quick fixes. This takes commitment and investment, of both our time and our presence.

We must go there.

Restoration is available although it will take work. It will take journeying. And it will take vulnerability.

So, given what you now know, will you set your heart on pilgrimage and recover what has been lost? Will you seek out the support that you need? Will you be brave enough to face the stories of harm that have crippled your creative capacity, and will you be patient enough to do the inner work that is necessary?

In summary, my big question to you is this: do you want to recover? *Really?*

I ask because there will be repercussions.

Whatever your own personal definition of artistic success is, becoming whole removes the excuse for not producing what you know you're capable of. The key will have been turned, the door unlocked, and you'll be free to step out from behind the bars. Of course, at this point, you can choose to create nothing at all, and that's okay, but you will have to own that freewill choice.

And not everyone will see or acknowledge the fierce effort you're making to become whole, yet they are likely to want some of the fruit you subsequently bear. Nor will everyone celebrate the fact you're starting to flourish. Envy from others is possible; probable, even. So, think carefully before choosing to pursue restoration from your Creative Wound. It will change you, and it will disturb the people who currently feature on the stage of your life. Some will even exit entirely, and you'll receive new players in their place. Or, as happened to Frodo Baggins, the Hobbit hero of Tolkien's *The Lord Of The Rings,* you may find that, after returning from your own epic journey of the heart, you are no longer at home within the confines of the small, safe world that was once all you knew. You will have grown so considerably, and seen so much, that you can never go back and be truly satisfied.

So, if restoration from your Creative Wound is what you desire, I suggest you begin by taking the journey through this book again, only more slowly. Don't take the train—ride your bike, or, better still, walk. Pause for as long as you need within the chapters that impact you the most, and give yourself the gift of time and space to process, and be nourished by, everything good and true that you discover.

I'm sure none of us ever wished to receive a Creative Wound. We never sought incidents of harm or abuse that would impede our creative confidence. But even though we received something difficult that we never consented to, we can make of it a grand adventure of discovery and restoration. And so, as you prepare to embark on your own pilgrimage, it is with a full and hope-filled heart that I sincerely wish you a most fruitful journey.

AUSTRALIAN MEMOIRS

The writing that got me back writing.

These are the short tales I refer to in the *Perfectionism & Play* chapter.

The Windsock

Today, we drove our campervan from near Wollongong to Canberra. This road had signs warning us of kangaroos, and I enthused at the prospect of seeing one in the wild for the first time.

As Sarah drove, I was the official kangaroo lookout—a role I felt confident in. Mile after mile passed but the only animals to pass before my eyes were cows. Lots of cows.

At one point I thought I'd spotted something about to make my fortune—a cow/kangaroo hybrid. I'd even invented a name for it—the "Kangamoo". It turned out to be a Llama.

As I grew weary at the lack of wildlife, a rather fetching windsock caught my eye.

So, to amuse myself, I started a silly discussion about taking a photograph of it when Sarah interrupted my waffle with a shout of "Kangaroo!" So, I frantically looked around. My eyes scoured every bit of the landscape. But they kept returning, as if magnetised, to the windsock. It had grabbed my attention and wouldn't let go.

So, Sarah saw our first kangaroo in the wild; and I saw a windsock. A bloody good windsock though. White, it was.

Fishballs

Have you heard it said, "The joy is in the journey"?

Well, that's not always true. Let me tell you a little story about our train trip to Sydney on Wednesday…

We'd become quite used to using the excellent Opal card service into Sydney (a little like the Oyster card in London). The trains have routinely been clean, quiet, on time, and superb value for money. I really like them, to be honest.

Wednesday's journey was the longest we'd taken into the city—about an hour long—and we boarded with our usual confidence.

However, the anticipated serenity broke when we were suddenly engulfed by a stench that rivalled the bowels of hell.

What on earth was *that?*

It wasn't just me who smelled it either. Up and down the carriage heads were turning. It was bad.

Then, I spotted her. The source seemed to be an unassuming middle-aged Chinese woman, sitting across the aisle and two seats up, the mouth of Hades surely open at her feet.

What *was* she doing?

Closer inspection revealed that said lady had seen fit, mid-journey, to dip into her shopping bag and open a plastic tub on her lap, in which resided what I can only surmise were three giant fish balls.

It was a curious sight. She didn't appear to have any designs on eating them. Instead, she seemed content to just cradle them in their Tupperware carry case, and gaze upon them with the intrigue and tenderness one might exhibit toward a cardboard box of newborn chicks.

This didn't last for seconds, either. Minutes passed, and on it went. The carriage filled with the aroma of this death fish as our friend two seats up contentedly sat tilting and rotating her little tub of precious deep-fried spheres. I guarantee you, never before has battered fish felt so cherished.

Now, far be it from me to criticise a lady for wanting to aerate her mammoth fish balls. I really don't resent her wanting to get a bit of breeze around them (after all, who wouldn't?) but surely there's a time and a place?

As I considered enlightening the woman about the improved entertainment she'd experience by swapping her a tub of fish balls for an iPhone, the train stopped and the driver announced we'd not be moving for a while…

Now, I wasn't sure if the delay was because of problems on the line or (hopefully) for the welcome relief of an emergency fumigation team about to burst in heroically and rescue us from this hideous poisson poisoning.

Unfortunately, it was the former.

At this point, fish ball lady cast a knowing glance our way then shared a huff and a puff of irritation at the delay. I wanted to reciprocate with the internationally recognised expression of disgust at the public airing of fish balls. But I didn't know it.

Eventually, the train set off again, only for the journey to be punctuated by more elongated stops as problems further down the line were attended to.

After what seemed like an eternity, the new public enemy of everyone in our carriage re-sealed her tub and placed it back in her bag. She'd not eaten a thing. Not even licked her fingers. Nothing. What on earth was that about?

A little light was then shed on my earlier wonderment about her phone. When she produced it from her bag, it was akin to something Del-Boy would have used circa 1985. I then suddenly felt compassion toward a woman who didn't carry Facebook around with her 24/7. What kind of life must she be enduring? If faced with this level of incomprehensible inhumanity, I might have chosen pet fish balls, too.

Never judge someone until you've walked a mile in their shoes.

As we proceeded, and the pungent odour slightly abated, the train public address system barked out a message for all those about to "Alight at Balls Head."

There'd have been a certain poetry to it if that had been fish ball lady's destination, but I concluded "Balls Head" was more likely the name of the medical condition now afflicting my brain following the prolonged stench.

As our most bizarre train journey neared its conclusion, at Sydney Town Hall, Sarah casually asked, "Where shall we go for lunch?"

Today, Chinatown wasn't an option.

Coffee Confusion

Buying a coffee from a coffee shop. I'm good at that. I *know* I am. I've done it hundreds of times.

So, I eased up to the barista's bar, and he asked, "How are you going?"

That threw me.

"Going?" I thought, "I've only just got here! Curious…"

So, I just smiled and glanced up to the coffee menu board above his head, to confirm my regular choice of an Americano.

There was no Americano. Hmmm…

All the other usual suspects appeared to be there, so by a process of elimination I concluded that "Long Black" is probably what I was after.

Good. So, what size do I want? Wait a minute—the

sizes are all different. In the UK, a tall drink is actually the smallest, but here tall actually means tall. Logical, maybe, but it added more complexity to the confusion in my pre-conditioned brain.

Something else then caught my eye. Flat whites are available in three sizes. What? As they're only available in one size in the UK (tall, their small) I'd equated the flat status with being small (maybe some kind of compression technique). A tall (actual tall, not our small tall) flat white seemed strange and new. What is this place?

All this was going on in my mind while the barista was still waiting to hear what method I'd be using to leave… My feet, perhaps?

The pressure was mounting, and I'd said nothing yet.

So, let's get this right. Tall is small, and large is tall and flat whites can be tall (not meaning the small tall, but the large tall) and Americanos are Long Blacks. Good.

So, what if I want milk with my (non-existent) Large Americano?

What do I actually want?

It seemed that I needed to ask for a "Tall White Long Black".

So, I'm about to ask for a drink that is black AND white. And it had to be tall AND long.

Just how elongated would it be? It sounded risky. It sounded like it could end up looking like a monochromatic barber's pole of a beverage. And nobody wants that, do they?

By now I felt a little self-conscious.

"Large cappuccino," I blurted. (I knew what that was, you see.)

Anyway, it's now a couple of weeks later as I reflect and write this little memoir; I'm over the worst of it now, and I've got myself a window seat in a lovely little cafe in Wagga Wagga. The aroma of freshly ground coffee is filling the air.

I'm having tea.

Sunday Curry

A Sunday curry has become a bit of a tradition of ours in the past couple of years. So, you can imagine our delight when our daily lunch hunt last Sunday led us to an Indian restaurant within minutes—and they even had a lunchtime special on!

The owner, Abdul, was a lovely, gracious man. Although his English was limited, we were all smiles as we took our seats in the centre of the restaurant and ordered our lunchtime special.

As I looked around the room I noticed that, curiously, every table had an industrial thickness plastic sheet on top of the tablecloth. However, the meals the other guests were eating looked wonderful; and so was ours when it arrived—even though we were surprised when it came served in a compartmentalised polystyrene tray with plastic forks!

It seemed we'd accidentally ordered from the takeaway

menu, and the language barrier had put a stop to any possible amendment from happening.

We all saw the funny side, though, and laughed even more when Abdul rushed to bring us knives, forks and spoons, and in his desperation to please, piled them high enough to service a small dinner party.

The food was very good though—some of the best we'd had so far. I finished mine off before Sarah, and so nipped off quickly to the loo.

The route there took me down a darkened corridor, which was hard to navigate after the brighter lighting of the restaurant. But, I did find the toilet ok. There it was, in an opening to the left. With no door.

Hmm… what's going on here?

I thought perhaps this toilet was out of order and one of the other two doors housed an actual functioning toilet.

So, I decided to have a look.

Fumbling for the handle in the twilight of the dimly lit corridor I successfully opened the door to the broom cupboard.

Oops. Not there, then.

One door remained. So, I had a look inside—the kitchen.

"Hello there! Nice job with the curry. Delicious!"

It turned out my first discovery had been right all along. I had to work this out. I'd seen other people go down this corridor and come back unscathed. I knew I could do this.

Quickly imagining what I thought Bear Grylls might do if faced with this dilemma, I concluded it a wise move to start by looking for a light switch.

I ran my hand along the walls and jumped as one of them moved! I investigated and was relieved to learn that I'd actually discovered the door: a sliding door, hidden in the dark, behind the wall. *What a good idea. I wondered why more people hadn't thought of that.*

By this point, I was getting a clearer picture of the terrain and soon located the light switch on the opposite wall. I turned it on, slid the door shut and locked myself in. All was finally well.

The toilet flush worked as expected, and I went over to the sink to wash my hands. I was now in more of a jovial mood, and liberally dispensed the liquid soap onto my hands then stuck them under the tap. Nothing happened.

So, I tried a few of my tried and trusted techniques. I waved my hands furiously. Slowly snuck up from the sides. Did side-to-side, and up-and-down motions; I even tried my 'mixing the pot' dance move. No water.

Not to be defeated, I looked for some kind of tap or switch. The sink was decorated with a cheap plastic plant in a pot, so I rotated this in the desperate hope it was Abdul's idea of a novelty fawcett. No such luck.

By now, I'd really had enough of this bathroom, and the swathes of gungy soap on my hands were congealing uncomfortably.

What I needed was a way of wiping it off. Toilet roll was the only option.

Now, for some reason, the bathroom designer had decided to fit the toilet roll holder down the side of the toilet, about three inches up from the skirting board. Being ever the polite sort, I didn't want to get soap all over the paper, so I leaned over to tear a sheet off using the sides of my hands. A difficult but noble manoeuvre. Balance was key here.

I tentatively bent further forward, a belly full of curry restricting my every move.

By the time my hand flanks finally reached the paper, my head was halfway down the pan and my southern hemisphere brazenly aloft.

Suddenly I heard a WHOOSH! Water? Water! The tap!

For no fathomable reason, the tap was now gushing lovely water—a mere six feet behind me. So, I darted across the room and thrust my hands into the sink, a split second after the water had stopped.

Frustrated, but with renewed hope, I tried a few more of my standard '70s disco and karate moves—using even more vigour than before, but I just couldn't get the tap to give up its water.

Finally admitting defeat, I concluded my dance of the digits with the least polite gesture I could muster, wiped most of the soap off, and trudged back to Sarah at our table.

"Are you alright? You've been gone a while," she chirped.

"I know you have trouble understanding toilets, but this one was so simple I knew you'd be ok!"

Please Leave A Review

If you enjoyed this book, please consider leaving a review on your favourite book website. Even a couple of sentences can make a big difference.

Also, if you know someone who would enjoy the read, please remember to tell them about *The Creative Wound*.

Thank you,
Mark

Acknowledgements

My heartfelt thanks go to:

My beautiful wife, Sarah, for believing in me with unswerving fierceness. Without your love and support, this book would never have happened.

Kyla, the apple of my eye. Here are a few things I've learned that I wish I'd known years earlier. I hope some of these thoughts from your old dad prove helpful.

My family, who continue to support me through it all.

The friends who journeyed with me, read the words I wrote, helped me process thoughts, cheered me on, and offered the brutally honest feedback I needed. Medals of honour go to Rob Pritchard, Tim Gough, Lauren Sapala, Rhian Atkin, Charlotte Bailey, Rick Jesse, Maggie Adams, Rebecca Hardie & Chelsea Moody.

Notes

Where Does The Art Go?

1. Date: October 4, 1976, Periodical: Time, Article: Modern Living: Ozmosis in Central Park, Note: The quotation appears as an epigraph at the beginning of the article. (Online archive of Time magazine) [Accessed on Dec. 2018]

2. 'A Japanese AI program just wrote a short novel, and it almost won a literary prize' (C. Olewitz, 2016) Available at: www.digitaltrends.com/cool-tech/japanese-ai-writes-novel-passes-first-round-nationanl-literary-prize [Accessed on Dec. 2018]

3. Pink, D. H. (2006). *A Whole New Mind: How To Thrive in the New Conceptual Age.* London: Cyan. (Introduction)

Creative Wound Stories

1. Allender, D. B. (2016). *Healing the Wounded Heart: The Heartache of Sexual Abuse and the Hope of Transformation.* Grand Rapids, MI: Baker Books, a division of the Baker Publishing Group. Kindle edition. (p. 58).

2. Van der Kolk, B. A. (2015). *The Body Keeps The Score: Mind, Brain and Body in the Transformation of Trauma.* London: Penguin Books. (p. 233).

The Clues Hidden In Your Story

1. Bly, R. (2015). *Iron John: A Book About Men.* Boston, MA: Da Capo Press. (p.30)

2. Chesterton, G.K. *The Scandal of Father Brown* (1935). Chapter 7.

Interpreting Our Stories

1. Anderson, K. (2016). *A Spirituality of Listening: Living What We Hear.* Downers Grove, IL: IVP Books, an imprint of InterVarsity Press. (p.100)

Passion & Choice

1. http://biblehub.com/greek/3958.htm [Accessed on Dec. 2018]

Good Ground

1. https://www.channel4.com/news/romania-tunnels-bucharest-orphans-photo [Accessed on Nov. 2018]

Thankful Thursday

1. See James 3:4

Meet You In Melbourne

1. https://www.facebook.com/urfruitful/ [Accessed on Nov. 2018]

Finish Something

1. Just 8% of People Achieve Their New Year's Resolutions. Here's How They Do It. www.forbes.com/sites/dandiamond/2013/01/01/just-8-of-people-achieve-their-new-years-resolutions-heres-how-they-did-it [Accessed on Sept. 2018]

2. York Minster www.historyofyork.org.uk/themes/york-minster [Accessed on Sept. 2018]

3. John Cage Organ Project in Halberstadt https://universes.art/magazine/articles/2012/john-cage-organ-project-halberstadt [Accessed on Sept. 2018]

Conclusion

1. How Fire Can Restore a Forest (Time lapse video)

https://blog.nature.org/conservancy/2013/07/24/how-fire-can-restore-a-forest-time-lapse-video [Accessed on Oct. 2018]

2. See Psalm 84:5-6

Bibliography

Allender, D. B., & Fann, L. K. (2005). *To Be Told Workbook: Know Your Story, Shape Your Life*. Colorado Springs, CO: Waterbrook Press.

Allender, D. B. (2016). *Healing the Wounded Heart: The Heartache of Sexual Abuse and the Hope of Transformation*. Grand Rapids, MI: Baker Books, a division of the Baker Publishing Group. Kindle edition.

Anderson, K. (2016). *A Spirituality of Listening: Living What We Hear*. Downers Grove, IL: IVP Books, an imprint of InterVarsity Press.

Bayles, D., & Orland, T. (2008). *Art & Fear: Observations on the Perils (and Rewards) of Artmaking*. Santa Cruz, CA: The Image Continuum.

Bell, R. (2017). *How To Be Here: A Guide To Creating a Life Worth Living*. London: William Collins.

Brown, B. (2018). *Braving The Wilderness: The Quest For True Belonging and the Courage to Stand Alone.* Farmington Hills, Mich: Thorndike Press

Cron, I. M. (2016). *The Road Back To You.* InterVarsity Press.

Gilbert, E. (2016). *Big Magic: Creative Living Beyond Fear.* London: Bloomsbury.

Gladwell, M. (2009). *Outliers.* Harmondsworth: Penguin.

Godin, S. (2014). *The Icarus Deception: How High Will You Fly?* London: Portfolio Penguin.

Godin, S. (2018). *Linchpin.* Little, Brown.

Herstand, A. (2016). *How To Make It in the New Music Business: Practical Tips on Building a Loyal Following and Making a Living as a Musician.* New York: Liveright Publishing Corporation.

Heuertz, C. L. (2017). *The Sacred Enneagram: Finding Your Unique Path To Spiritual Growth.* Grand Rapids, MI: Zondervan.

Judkins, R. (2016). *The Art Of Creative Thinking: 89 Ways to See Things Differently.* New York: Perigee, an imprint of Penguin Random House LLC.

Leaf, C. (2018). *Switch On Your Brain: The Key to Peak Happiness, Thinking, and Health.* Baker Book House.

McManus, E. R. (2015). *The Artisan Soul: Crafting Your Life Into a Work of Art.* San Francisco: HarperOne.

Medina, J., Medina, J. J., Pearson, M. R., & Stevenson, R. W. (2008). *Brain Rules.* Pear Press.

Moyle, F. (2016). *Turner: The Extraordinary Life And Momentous Times Of J.M.W. Turner.* London: Penguin.

Newport, C. (2016). *Deep Work.* London: Piatkus.

Nordby, J. (2016). *Blessed Are The Weird: A Manifesto For Creatives.* Boise, ID: Manifesto Publishing House.

Pink, D. H. (2018). *Drive: The Surprising Truth About What Motivates Us.* S.l.: Canongate Books.

Pink, D. H. (2006). *A Whole New Mind: How To Thrive in the New Conceptual Age.* London: Cyan.

Sapala, L. (2016). *The INFJ Writer: Cracking The Creative Genius Of The World's Rarest Type.* San Francisco, CA: Lauren Sapala.

Thompson, C. (2010). *Anatomy of the Soul: Surprising Connections Between Neuroscience and Spiritual Practices That Can Transform Your Life and Relationships.* Carol Stream, IL: Tyndale House.

Van der Kolk, B. A. (2015). *The Body Keeps The Score: Mind, Brain and Body in the Transformation of Trauma.* London: Penguin Books.

About The Author

Mark Pierce is a creative professional who has spent over 25 years working in the sweet spot where photography, design, and music collide. He lives in North Wales, UK, with his wife and daughter.

You can read more of Mark's notes on the creative life at **www.markpiercewriter.com**, or feel free to check out his studio work website, which is **www.revelator.co.uk**.

If you need an antidote to creative block, you might like to sign up for his mailing list and get **Unstick Quick!** – a free three-part course designed to get your creativity flowing again, *fast*.

Get the course at **www.markpiercewriter.com/unstick**

Printed in Great Britain
by Amazon